THE PERSON

OF THE

HOLY SPIRIT

WHO IS HE, ANYWAY?

GLORY CHAPMAN

SP

**SOUTHWICK PUBLISHING
HOUSTON, TEXAS**

TABLE OF CONTENTS

Chapter

1	WHO IS HE, ANYWAY?
2	WHAT IS HIS PURPOSE FOR BEING HERE?
3	CONSCIENCE
4	THE WORK OF THE HOLY SPIRIT
5	ATTRIBUTES OF THE HOLY SPIRIT
6	NAMES OF THE HOLY SPIRIT
7	H.S. CARRIES THE VOICE OF THE FATHER
8	HOLY SPIRIT GIVES HOPE AND COMFORT
9	H. S. BRINGS US INTO GOD'S PRESENCE
10	H.S. HELPS IN PRAYER AND INTERCESSION
11	FRUITS OF THE HOLY SPIRIT
12	THE HOLY SPIRIT GIVES GIFTS

THE PERSON OF THE HOLY SPIRIT

Chapter 1

WHO IS HE, ANYWAY?

Number one, the Holy Spirit is the most famous author who ever lived and still lives. His book has out sold all other books and continues to be the perennial best-seller today--the Holy Bible! It is known as the *indestructible book* due to the many attempts to destroy it over many centuries. There were men who were martyred for putting the Scripture into the language of the common people. It is God's Word (God-breathed). "For no prophecy recorded in Scripture was ever thought up by the prophet himself. It was the Holy Spirit within these godly men who gave them true messages from God." 2 Peter 1:21,22.

Along with being the most famous author, He is also the most misunderstood person in all the world, other than Jesus Christ.

As to how He got to earth, the person of the Holy Spirit was a going-away gift that Jesus Christ gave to the world when he ascended back to His Father in heaven after the resurrection. He gave us a personal guide who would lead us home if we always followed Him--no matter the circumstances. Now the Holy Spirit would be *inside* each one of us. That's how close Jesus wanted his gift to be at all times--constant availability.

But it seems man has always had a problem understanding his Creator God, Jesus His Son and the person of the Holy Spirit. Sure proof that God has opposition in trying to keep us blinded from the truth--the devil.

Can I propose that we clear our minds of much misinformation and denominational doctrine? Just simply clear our minds of any prejudice and heresay, and open our hearts fully to what the person of the Holy Spirit would want us to learn about Himself. We are inquirers endeavoring to ask the Holy Spirit to reveal to us more fully the person of Jesus Christ, and to show us better how to worship our Savior. But first it is imperative that we open wide our heart's door for the Holy Spirit to enter. He only comes when we give Him our consent or permission.

This study was prompted by the many strange remarks I kept hearing about the person of the Holy Spirit. Certainly, not everyone is going to agree on every point, but this exploration is not to draw us into arguments or debates, but rather to enlighten us as to who the Holy Spirit really is, and get to know Him on an intimate basis. I am awed by what I have learned! What a magnificent gift Jesus asked the Father to give us—A PERSONAL GUIDE FOR EACH INDIVIDUAL BELIEVER IF THE HOLY SPIRIT IS GIVEN AN INVITATION AND WELCOME.

He is the *third person* of the Trinity, never an *'it'*. He is Spirit also, just as God is, and God says we are to worship Him in spirit and in truth. <u>**HE IS THE ONLY PERSON OF THE GODHEAD WHO IS ON EARTH TO HELP US. THE FATHER AND JESUS ARE IN HEAVEN.**</u> If God sent His Holy Spirit to earth as a gift to us, and we choose to ignore Him, don't make His acquaintance or welcome Him into our hearts, how do you think God views that attitude? If the Holy Spirit is God---then are we not spurning God Himself?

THE PERSON OF THE HOLY SPIRIT

Just as the world was disbelieving (or ignorant) of God's *Son* when God sent Him to earth, so much of the church today is disbelieving in the person of the Holy Spirit, whom God sent. Do we not realize that the Holy Spirit can do better and far surpassing things for us than we are capable of doing for ourselves?

Charles Stanley in *The Wonderful Spirit-Filled Life* emphasizes it this way: "When Christ was crucified, there was no longer any need for the temple. God no longer needed a building. He was free to take up residence in the heart of man. Paul refers to believers as temples—God had changed His residence for good. He had left the temple in Jerusalem and, through the person of the Holy Spirit, had moved into the hearts of his people *upon invitation.*

"Haven't you yet learned that your body is the home of the Holy Spirit God gave you, and that He lives *within* you? Your own body does not belong to you." I Cor. 6:19

I love how R. A. Torrey in his book, *The Holy Spirit,* explains it, "So it is clear that every regenerate man has the Holy Spirit. But in many a believer the Holy Spirit dwells away back in some hidden sanctuary of his person, away back of conscious experience. So just as it is one thing to have a guest in your house living in some remote corner of the house where you scarcely know that he is there, and quite another thing to have the guest taking entire possession of the house, just so it is one thing to have the Holy Spirit dwelling way back of consciousness in some hidden sanctuary of our being, and quite another thing to have the Holy Spirit taking entire possession of the house.

"In other words, it is one thing to have the Holy Spirit merely dwelling in us but we are not conscious of His dwelling, and quite another thing to be filled with the Holy Spirit. So we may put it with perfect accuracy in this way: Every regenerate person has the Holy Spirit, but not every regenerate person has what the Bible calls being *filled with the Holy Spirit.*

"The real challenge comes in how to get the Holy Spirit out of the 'hidden sanctuary' and into our daily activities. We obviously are going to need some empowering and guidance if we are going to fulfill our destiny. The first place to start is get to the end of ourselves, even to a point of desperation where we are so sick of ourselves and our inability to change that we throw up our hands in surrender. Have you noticed that is when many people find Christ--in desperate circumstances?"

Torrey goes on to say that the phrases *filled with the Spirit, baptized by the Spirit, the gift of the Spirit, the Holy Spirit fell upon them, and endued with power from on high* all refer to the same experience, an experience that generally occurs sometime after regeneration.

"As soon as they arrived, they began praying for these new Christians to receive the Holy Spirit, for as yet he had not come upon any of them. For they had only been baptized in the name of the Lord Jesus. Then Peter and John laid their hands upon these believers, and they received the Holy Spirit." Acts 8:15-17.

According to Charles Stanley, "More people discover the wonderful Spirit-filled life in the valley than in any other

THE PERSON OF THE HOLY SPIRIT

place. God uses sickness, financial pressure, appetites, habits, children, work, whatever it takes. Because once He finally has our attention, He knows the best is yet to come.

"God is an expert at engineering circumstances so that we find ourselves with nowhere to turn but to Him. In His wisdom He knows that some of us must be pushed to the brink of disaster before we come to the place mentally, emotionally, and spiritually where we throw in the towel and entrust ourselves fully to the God who created us."

Have we come to the place in our life of total dependence and total surrender to God, thus making it possible for the Holy Spirit to maximize His work in our life?

The filling of the Spirit is something that takes place in accordance with our willingness to surrender to the influence of the Spirit. "And be not drunk with wine, wherein is excess; but be filled with the Spirit" (Eph. 5:18). What we may miss in this passage is--to be drunk is to be under the control of alcohol, to surrender one's body, mind, and spirit to its influence. To be filled with the Spirit--in this particular case--is to voluntarily put one's self under the influence of the Holy Spirit even as a drunkard is dominated and controlled by his intoxicating wine.

How does one become drunk with wine? By drinking and spending time with the bottle. We need to spend time drinking in the Word and meditating, filling our thoughts about Him until we *fall in love* and have a *passion* for Him, then we are saturated and full of His presence. In His presence is where we are changed forever!

If we can be full, then it seems possible that we could also be empty at times! Consider Elijah, Jonah, John Mark, and Peter, to name a few. We need to ask ourselves, if we are half full, what is filling our other half?

"Those who believe Him discover that God is a fountain of truth. For this one--sent by God--speaks God's words, for God's Spirit is upon him *without measure or limit.*" John 3:34

The Spirit-filled life is a life of faith--not a formula--but a relationship controlled by the person of the Holy Spirit. By His power we are able to love what God loves and hate what God hates.

In studying who the Holy Spirit is, we are going to be addressing God's Spirit and the Holy Spirit as it pertains to our spirit part--*all invisible* members. As you know, we are made up of the *body* (physical), *soul* (intellect, will and emotion) and a *spirit.* We are born physically with a carnal, unregenerate human spirit. Now the Bible says we have to be born another time---the spirit part of us, and be adopted and made a part of God's family through accepting what His Son, Jesus Christ, did for us in dying on the cross for our sins. In this acceptance, we are given a new heart and nature, and are welcomed as a new baby into God's own family.

As a new baby Christian, we should have a healthy appetite for learning, growing and maturing. Upon reaching each stage of growth, we should actively be participating in God's family, contributing something, however little. *Find our place in the family of God and function in the gifts and*

THE PERSON OF THE HOLY SPIRIT

opportunities given us. In other words, find out for what purpose we were created. With the Holy Spirit as a guide and teacher, we should flow and fulfill our destiny in life as He planned and scheduled it.

"You saw me before I was born and scheduled each *day* of my life before I began to breathe. Every day was recorded in your Book!" Psa. 139:16

We can learn and learn with the intellect, but this study is to help us learn about the <u>Holy Spirit and our spirit</u> and how they relate. <u>Unless the Holy Spirit touches our spirit, usually spiritual things have little real meaning to us.</u> We hear and know but can't seem to appropriate its truth. The Holy Spirit and our spirit must be able to communicate in meaningful ways with each other. We start with the mind, but at some point what we learn must be translated into our spirit, which in turn moves us to action. *Until Spirit to spirit is connecting, it is still in the head,* and all that is produced at this level is legalism and sad Christianity because it does not change our hearts. We are trudging along under our own steam and it is so dreary and dreadful--hardly a sunbeam anywhere.

Many a tireless, nervous body has driven a spirit. The spirit should be the master always. This means no worry, no anxiety, but it does not mean no effort. The man who reaches the mountain height by the help of train or car has learned no climber's lesson.

We can not expect God to ease the burdens we choose to carry.

GLORY CHAPMAN

Do you know any sad unfulfilled Christians? It's not so much *abstaining* from sins as it is our being filled with the Holy Spirit who helps and enables us to overcome evil in our lives. *And the overcoming is never the overcoming of the one who troubles us, but the overcoming of the weaknesses and wrong in our own nature, aroused by such a one.* Somehow we haven't been able to fall in-love with Christ. We've talked, reasoned and analyzed, even hoped and prayed, yet the love is not there. It's so hard, so confusing, so difficult, so disappointing, but we keep trying our best. It's definitely the hard way.

Knowing a person is synonymous with spending time with that person.

Perhaps we haven't spent enough time with the Holy Spirit to fall in-love. Charles Stanley says that simply going through the motions--going to church, reading the Bible, saying prayers and confessing our sins--is not where the joy is. Our lives and marriages are filled with everything but the Spirit--no peace, joy and love. If the Christian life is merely trying to do our best, there was no need for God to send the Holy Spirit to help us. *Obviously, God knew we would need help in an evil and perverse world to overcome.* Our spirits need to be awakened and brought to life by the Holy Spirit so He can do the generating and empowering (putting fire in our bellies as it were). He has to be the one pushing the wagon. Our strength is all too weak and human, whereas His strength is strong, everlasting and supernatural.

Jack Taylor said that his father was a very good farmer, and that he simply deduced that if his father could become a

THE PERSON OF THE HOLY SPIRIT

good farmer by hard work, he could become a good Christian in the same manner. It's impossible to live the Christian life successfully without the ENERGY of the Holy Spirit infusing us.

My dad was a good example of trying to be a Christian by trying and trying. It seemed he could only push so long. The hill was too steep! That's why the Father chose to send the Holy Spirit to earth to walk *alongside* us and be *in* us. Otherwise, He knew we would never make it on our own. <u>We would sooner be without clothing and food than without the person of the Holy Spirit. That's how important He is!</u>

Hopefully, at the point we give our lives to Christ, we are not marrying Him for His money, benefits and protection. What man would want a girl to marry him only for his money? Yet that is what we do if we are not properly taught and given responsibilities in our early training. We expect God to be our Santa Claus without our contributing anything towards the relationship. Is that healthy in any situation---spiritual or in the natural?

To be perfectly honest, I grew up trying to keep God's commandments, attending church very, very often, paying tithes, and I had the notion I was at the top of the list for the Rapture. Certainly, I don't want to judge others by myself, but it seems from what I can observe, many feel betrayed by God because He doesn't come through for them like they want. Kind of like a teenager who wants a red Corvette and doesn't get it. He gets bent all out of shape because his parents won't cooperate. Do we not have some commitment and responsibility?

GLORY CHAPMAN

What has our love for Christ and His gift of the Holy Spirit caused us to do for the benefit in *His* kingdom?

This gives me pause, and I am still trying to figure out where I fit in His great big family. Wow! Perhaps it is better late than never, but where have I been? Guess I had only been counting on all *my benefits,* feeling that God was big and didn't need anything from me.

When I was teaching on "prayer" this principle hit me full force. I was asking, begging, cajoling, coercing God with my want-list continuously. Then it dawned on me, w*hat was I giving back to Him on a daily basis?* Where was my love, appreciation and devotion for Him? Hard to get those kinds of petitions through to the Holy Spirit, who in turn gives them to our advocate, Jesus, who in turn gives them to the Father, who answers them according to His will. I dare say those prayers of mine probably died very short deaths.

I have known and learned from childhood about the Scriptures, the rules, regulations, and parables, but what I missed was God's Holy Spirit reaching into my invisible spirit revealing to me *what Jesus Christ did for me* personally. Sort of like drawing a picture in my spirit. Remember the Holy Spirit always unveils, reveals, makes plain, shows us the tremendous amazing love that Christ has for us. He enhances our view and opinion of the person of Jesus the Messiah.

Until we came to Christ, Paul tells us in Ephesians 2:1, "And you were dead (spiritually) in your trespasses and

THE PERSON OF THE HOLY SPIRIT

sins."

My spirit needs to be melded with God's Holy Spirit. When I am birthed for the second time, my spiritual eyes are opened and I am made *alive* unto God, making it possible for me to follow His plan for my life, because He is infusing me minute-by-minute, and hour-by-hour. *His power and life in me makes it possible for me to do His will.* Otherwise, my natural and fleshly desires tend to overrule my spirit and take charge.

The Holy Spirit Imparts Power

Jesus speaking just before He ascended, "But when the Holy Spirit has come upon you, you will receive **power** to testify about me with great effect, to the people in Jerusalem, throughout Judea, in Samaria, and to the ends of the earth, about my death and resurrection." Acts 1:8

Remember Peter denied knowing Jesus while He was being crucified, but after Peter was filled with the Holy Spirit 50 days later, he preached with such power that 3,000 people were saved at his first sermon.

Do we need the power of the Holy Spirit to anoint our words in telling others about Jesus, or can we be effective enough with our own vocabulary?

Dr. Luke wrote, "Then he was filled with the joy of the Holy Spirit and said, "I praise you, O Father, Lord of heaven and earth, for hiding these things from the intellectuals and worldly wise and for revealing them to those who are as trusting as little children. Yes, thank you,

Father, for that is the way you wanted it." Luke 10:21

Paul tells us in Gal. 5:16, "I advise you to obey only the Holy Spirit's instructions. He will *tell you where to go and what to do,* and then you won't always be doing the wrong things your evil nature wants you to. For we naturally love to do evil things that are just the opposite from the things that the Holy Spirit tells us to do; . . .These two forces within us are constantly fighting each other to win control over us, and our wishes are never free from their pressures."

THE PERSON OF THE HOLY SPIRIT

CHAPTER 2

WHAT IS HIS PURPOSE FOR BEING HERE?

Why Did God Send the Holy Spirit to our Planet?

Jesus said, "But I tell you the truth, it is to your advantage that I go away; for if I do not go away, the Helper shall not come to you; but if I go, I will send Him (Holy Spirit) to you." John 16:7 NAS.

Why is it that man prefers to follow some person, doctrine or accepted theology before he accepts what the Scriptures say about the Holy Spirit? This puzzles me. The Holy Spirit wrote the Scriptures (within these godly men who gave them true messages from God). Why not ask the author about what He wrote? What better authority is there? In reading a book recently on the different points of view about the Bible, it seems man has always had divisive thoughts about God, and tries to improve on what the Holy Spirit wrote, and in doing so, have led people into many denominations, even into cults.

What keeps Christians from calling upon the Holy Spirit direct? Notice, I said Christians. Certainly we need to fellowship with other Christians and go to church, but there is no one who can keep us from worshipping God in our hearts. No one! **Nicki Rowe from McAllen, Texas,** who wrote, *Five Years to Freedom,* was a prisoner of war in

Vietnam longer than any other prisoner at that time. He said that the Vietcong had put him in a bamboo cage and tied him spread eagle on the ground for months at a time. He could not even scratch himself from all the mosquito bites or get up to go to the bathroom. He had no Bible, no pencil or paper. They took everything away from him, but there was one thing they couldn't touch and that was his spirit. He still had his faith and could worship God as much as he liked. That was enough to keep him alive under the most outrageous circumstances possible. The Holy Spirit helped him and the other prisoners to remember the words to the *Old Rugged Cross,* and parts of Scripture they had learned when they were in Sunday School years before.

No one can hinder us from singing hymns and psalms, clapping our hands, laughing, reading, and praying. Worship is a very private and personal thing between each man and his God. Everyday we are to be filling up with the Holy Spirit, not necessarily in church. We are to arrive full and be ready to contribute to others. We are to use our gifts to bless others and help build up God's kingdom. Read the whole chapter of I Cor. 14.

Do you suppose one or two meals of food a week would be sufficient to keep us vibrant and healthy, either physically or spiritually?

"The Holy Spirit came to reside in men's hearts through being *birthed again* (regeneration) and to be everywhere at once whereas the person of Jesus Christ in the flesh could only be at one place at a time. There would be more of us to do His works throughout the world.

THE PERSON OF THE HOLY SPIRIT

<u>What is His Purpose for Being Here?</u>

He was sent to draw men. "No man can come to me, except the Father which hath sent me draw him;..." John 6:44; also to restrain evil and help Christians, inciting us to good actions, as well as to convict us of sin. Conscience in the natural man is inoperative unless stirred up by the Spirit to illuminate our hearts. This is very evident from the state of the heathen.

The Holy Spirit is first a witness for Christ, also empowering us to be His witnesses to a lost world. Jesus explained, "When the Helper comes, whom I will send to you from the Father, that is the Spirit of truth, who proceeds from the Father, He will bear witness of Me, and you will bear witness also, because you have been with Me from the beginning." John 15:26,27. NAS

First, let's establish how we read the Bible *Do we read what we believe, or do we believe what we read?* We don't need to read into the text more than is there. If we read with an agenda, our findings will always be suspect. Read with the context in mind, not using isolated verses. In our study of the person of the Holy Spirit, we may need to go back in each lesson and read the entire chapter or book to understand the whole context in which it was written and to whom. Why is it dangerous to look for a special message from God by opening the Bible at random and reading a verse out of context? I did this once and my finger fell on the Scripture, "And He said to him, 'Truly I say to you, today you shall be with Me in Paradise.'" Luke 23:43 NAS. However, if the Holy Spirit impressed upon you to look at a particular Scripture, that is different.

What is the first word or thought that comes to your mind when I say, *Holy Spirit?*

Think about it for a minute! Over the last few years, I have heard some strange comments about the person of the Holy Spirit. Clearly, we are misinformed in some instances. Let's look at Scripture and see if we can secure a very clear view of His person, work and character.

"Much ignorance prevails today concerning the Holy Spirit. The Old Testament saints had far more in common with the New Testament saints than is generally supposed. A verse which has been grossly perverted by many of our moderns is John 7:39, "The Holy Spirit was not yet given, because that Jesus was not yet glorified." The words 'was not yet given' can no more be understood absolutely than 'Enoch was not' (Gen. 5:24); they simply mean that the Spirit had not yet been given in His full administrative authority. He was not yet publicly manifested here on earth. All believers, in every age, had been sanctified and comforted by Him, but the *ministration of the Spirit* (II Cor. 3:8) was not at that time fully introduced; the outpouring of the Spirit, in the plentitude of His miraculous gifts, had not then taken place." *The Holy Spirit* by Arthur W. Pink, page 22. It is a mistake to say that the Holy Spirit was never in any believer before Pentecost. Read Numbers 27:18; Neh. 9:30; I Peter 1:11; Acts 7:51; Zech. 4:6; II Cor. 4:13; Ezek. 2:2; Dan. 1:17; Jer. 1:5; Isa. 1:1.

Timing is so important in God's plan for mankind, and always has been down through the ages. If our spirit can link up with the Holy Spirit's, then we can relax and let Him

THE PERSON OF THE HOLY SPIRIT

unfold *what* our purpose is and *when* it is to be. It might be His plan that we should marry someday, but not at age five! Timing! Timing! Timing! His timing! Also, a kindergarten student is not yet ready to become superintendent of schools!

"Isn't it interesting to note that Jesus was <u>first anointed</u> in His mother's womb? His humanity was endowed with all spiritual graces, and through childhood and up to the age of 30 He was guided and preserved by the Holy Spirit. Upon His <u>second anointing</u>, He was formally consecrated unto His public mission and Divinely endowed for His official work. This took place at the River Jordan--the heavens opened, the Holy Spirit descended upon Him in the form of a dove, and the voice of the Father was heard. Matt. 3:16,17. The first work was personal and private, the latter being official and public; the one was bestowing upon Him of spiritual graces, the other imparting to Him ministerial gifts. Christ's <u>third anointing</u> was reserved for his exaltation--an ascension gift." Arthur W. Pink, page 26. Notice the time plan?

In watching a documentary about the Royal Family recently on television, I was so surprised to know that at Queen Elizabeth II's Coronation, she was anointed with oil by the Bishop of the Church of England, and that the gifts of the Holy Spirit were bestowed upon her. The ceremony for this was so sacred it was not permitted to be photographed. Queen Elizabeth is the Head of the Church of England. What a responsibility!

<u>The Bible Says The Holy Spirit is a *Person*, *N*ever an *'It'*</u>.

He is the third *person* of the Godhead. He is fully God and fully Jesus Christ. The Trinity perhaps can be explained thus--One God in three persons with three different functions like a minister could be a husband, a father, a brother, a son, an employee, a friend, but he is only one person with many functions. Does that help?

"John replied, "God in heaven appoints each man's work..." John 3:27. Have we self-appointed ourselves as to what work we will do in life? Could that be why so many are unhappy with what they are doing?

<ins>The Holy Spirit Can Be Likened to an In-House Tutor.</ins>

There is nothing He doesn't know, but to transfer His knowledge to us, we have to consult or ask Him. A teacher may stand in the front of the class and ask if the students have questions to come forward, and she will be glad to help them. If the students never open their mouths or verbalize what they need or want to know, how much help will be forthcoming? Wouldn't it have been grand in school to have had a tutor or teacher who knew all the answers and could have relayed them to us 24 hours a day--especially at test time? Wow!

Spirit-filled believers come to the Scriptures with teachable spirits. They don't view Bible study as simply a fact-finding mission, or from an intellectual viewpoint. They see it as an opportunity to peer into the mind and heart of God.

I was appalled when I discovered how little I could verbalize as to the person, character and work of the Holy Spirit in a meaningful way to someone else.

THE PERSON OF THE HOLY SPIRIT

Jesus said, "I will ask the Father, and He will give you another Helper, that He may be with you forever." John 14:16. He also said, "I will not leave you as orphans; I will come to you." John 14:18. Is this not proof of Jesus' further love and concern for us?

However, to experience His person, power and presence, I must invite Him into my life because God gave us free wills to choose His kingdom or the kingdom of Satan. God is not going to violate our free will and force us to do the right thing. *I must have a longing, a passion for Him.* As I open my heart fully to the Holy Spirit, He then pours His *presence* out in a real and tangible way. Broken lives are healed because of His presence and we are changed forever. He manifests His presence and power to those who yearn for His touch upon their lives. *Spiritual thirst draws His anointing like a siphon draws fluid from a full container to an empty one.*

The Holy Spirit wants to be a permanent resident in our hearts--not a guest or a visitor from time to time.

Perhaps *passion* can be explained like this. It's like falling in-love with the man of our dreams. Were we not consumed with compelling thoughts of joy, thrilled at his closeness, and oh, that look of love that melted us with that feeling of security that led us into a total commitment for a lifetime? We could literally spend endless hours we were so enthralled with love for our beloved. The other side of that coin is we could marry someone for whom we have no *passion, marrying for the wrong reasons,* and life would indeed be hard with no joy and in-loveness to propel and motivate us through the years.

Without the Holy Spirit helping us, we are incapable of falling in-love with Christ; That's why He is such an important Person..

The Holy Spirit keeps reminding us of the imminent return of Christ and that He is coming for those who are looking for Him. We need this daily prompting to keep us focused on eternal things. This world has so many distractions-- maybe more now than any other generation. We are bombarded with many choices, opportunities and options. We need someone to keep us on track, and the person of the Holy Spirit was sent with that in mind.

"I will pour water on him who is thirsty, and floods on the dry ground; I will pour My Spirit on your descendants, and My blessing on your offspring." Isa. 44:3.

Only those who *yearn* to know the Lord and who *yield* to Him in *faith* will experience His power and His work in their life. In life, we often put our faith in things we don't understand. Flying in a jet airplane, we place our lives in the hands of people we have never met and are at the mercy of machinery we don't understand. That is not to imply that nobody understands it simply because I don't. Why is it so difficult for us to have faith in God and his gifts? Why? It would almost seem we are suspicious of these at times. We don't understand and neither can we unless we are born of the Spirit because they are spiritually discerned. Our spirit part has to become *alive* first.

<u>We Are to be Led by the Spirit.</u>

THE PERSON OF THE HOLY SPIRIT

"For all who are led by the Spirit of God are sons of God." Rom. 8:14. As Charles Stanley puts it, if we are to be led by the Spirit (Gal. 5:18), it would certainly help if we could recognize Him! It is very difficult to follow someone whose identity is unknown. He has been sent to assist us in all the practical matters of Christian living. We must get to know Him intimately--talk to Him. Thank Him. The Spirit-filled life is a life characterized by keeping in step with the Holy Spirit. Our relationship should be so close that we recognize his voice and promptings. How close do lovers stay? *Love can survive almost any blow except one, and that is, neglect.* Remember any relationship has to be nurtured constantly to keep it alive!

We have to be continuously filled. One filling won't last long. How long will one meal last?

"If we are living now by the Holy Spirit's power, let us follow the Holy Spirit's leading in every part of our lives." Gal. 5:25.

It is Imperative That We Have an Understanding of His Personhood.

He is a *person*. He's not a force or an influence. Only when we understand that can we appropriate His work. He has intellect, emotion and will. Many live their lives as if He were a force instead of a person. We will never advance beyond a certain level in our Christian life until we truly come to grips with the fact that the *Holy Spirit thinks, feels, communicates, perceives and responds. He gives and receives love. He grieves when He has been ignored.* We can know this person. He will be our beloved companion *upon invitation.*

We Must Ask For the Holy Spirit:

Jesus speaking, "If ye then, being evil, know how to give good gifts unto your children: how much more shall your heavenly **Father give the Holy Spirit to them that ask him?"** Luke 11:13. KJV

When the Spirit comes into our lives, above all, He longs to have fellowship with us and to bring us into the very presence of His Father, God Almighty. When we know the Holy Spirit, the more we know the Father and the Son because the Holy Spirit never exalts Himself but always magnifies the Lord Jesus. *He doesn't seek His own glory, nor does He want to draw attention to Himself, but to Jesus.* He longs to reveal Jesus to us and empower us to love Him with all our heart, soul, and strength. But for that to happen, we must welcome Him into our life.

Just as God sent His Son to earth to show man what God was like, so Jesus asked the Father to send the Holy Spirit to earth to be personally *within* each of us to show us what God and Jesus are like. Not only that but **He gives us His power to become more Christlike.** Otherwise, the natural man is severely limited in beholding and recognizing the ways of God. Spirit communes with spirit -- the physical to the physical.

The best way to express our love to the Lord Jesus is to surrender and be totally dependent upon the Holy Spirit every day. That is absolutely essential if we are to know the

THE PERSON OF THE HOLY SPIRIT

person of the Holy Spirit. However, surrender is only possible through prayer and brokenness before the Lord. In our society the word *dependent* does not have a good connotation, does it? In our physical world, it is not a good thing, but in the spiritual realm, it is not only imperative but when we are totally dependent upon the Holy Spirit is when He does His greatest and best for us. When I am at my weakest, He is at His strongest. When I am at my worst, He is at His best! That way we know it was God and God alone who acted on our behalf. We must always be aware of the difference between the physical and the spiritual realms. Its principles are like the symbol of the cross--+--opposites.

Charles Stanley states, "That the Spirit-filled life begins once we are absolutely convinced that we can do nothing apart from the indwelling strength of the Holy Spirit. Until that one simple truth grips us at the core of our being, we will never experience the full-blown power of the Holy Spirit. Why? Because we will always be out there doing things *for* God in our strength. And when we fail, we will promise to do better next time. Without meaning to, many Christians live independently of the Holy Spirit every day. They never give Him a second thought, much less consult Him on issues both great and small."

It's a mystery we get through life as well as we do with so little help--mostly by pulling ourselves up by our own bootstraps. God has grander plans for us and sent Someone to instruct and tutor us. Could we be like the man aboard ship eating cheese and crackers, not realizing his ticket afforded him delicious meals and sumptuous midnight buffets?

Hence the reason to be informed. "Study to show thyself approved unto God, a workman that needeth not to be ashamed, rightly dividing the word of truth." 2 Tim. 2:15.

THE PERSON OF THE HOLY SPIRIT

Chapter 3

CONSCIENCE

<u>The Conscience and the Holy Spirit.</u>

Everyone has a conscience. ". . . God's laws are written within them; their own conscience accuses them, or sometimes excuses them." Rom. 2:12-15 "For the truth about God is known to them instinctively; God has put this knowledge in their hearts." Rom. 1:19

The Holy Spirit uses the conscience as a primary avenue of communication. The term *conscience* appears 30 times in the New Testament. The conscience is that inner capacity within each of us to discern right from wrong, wise from unwise. It functions as a megaphone in the hands of the Holy Spirit. Paul speaking, "I tell the truth in Christ, I am not lying, my conscience also bearing me witness in the Holy Spirit, that I have great sorrow and continual grief in my heart." Rom. 9:1-2 NKJV.

When you became a Christian, the Spirit of truth took up residence in your heart, and set about to complete the programming of your conscience. Whereas before you had a general sense of right and wrong, the Holy Spirit began renewing your mind to more specific and complete truths. (see I Cor. 2:10-13).

". . .So we use the Holy Spirit's words to explain the Holy

Spirit's facts. But the man who isn't a Christian can't understand and can't accept these thoughts from God, which the Holy Spirit teaches us. They sound foolish to him, because only those who have the Holy Spirit within them can understand what the Holy Spirit means. Others just can't take it in." Rom. 2:13-14.

The Holy Spirit uses the conscience as an instant warning device. Paul tells us, "And now, compelled by the Spirit, I am going to Jerusalem, not knowing what will happen to me there. I only know that in every city *the Holy Spirit warns me* that prison and hardships are facing me." Acts 20:22-23. NIV.

For several years during the bad part of my life, a certain song would just zoom in on my conscience, and it was always a warning that something else bad was going to happen. It was the song, *Jesus, Savior Pilot Me*. It was both fearful and reassuring at the same time.

The conscience, once it is empowered by the Holy Spirit, can correctly discern or evaluate what is and what is not of God. Spirit-consciousness replaces sight.

The Holy Spirit uses the conscience to convict and convince us of sin. Peter viewed the conscience as a trustworthy indicator of the presence or absence of sin. I Peter 3:15-16. Paul also wrote about conscience in 2 Cor. 1:12.

Don't ignore the warnings and promptings of the conscience. A clear conscience is evidence of a life in harmony with the Holy Spirit. That is what the Spirit-filled life is all about.

THE PERSON OF THE HOLY SPIRIT

The question is not, "Do I have a certain gift?" The question is, "Can I surrender all to Him?"

It is then that He begins to reveal Himself and His love for us. And a fellowship begins that grows and intensifies until we say, "Lord Jesus, I give You my life, my mind, my heart, my dreams, my emotions, my thoughts; I give them all to You. I surrender spirit, soul (mind) and body. It is then that the Holy Spirit begins to teach us about all that the Father has for us." John 14:26. As Isaiah declared, "In quietness and in confidence shall be your strength." 30:15.

Now we will begin to experience the *presence* of the Holy Spirit. We are now aware *He is inside us,* walking alongside as a helper. He never leaves us if we don't grieve or quench Him. He stays ever so close to those who desire His company--wherever we are. He is waiting for us to extend an invitation that we want and desire Him. We must give Him the right to enter our spirit. At that point, we are power launched into interaction with our permanent in-house tutor. What greater security could we possibly know?

If it is as simple as that, then why doesn't everyone rush to this truth? Jesus speaking, "The world's sin is unbelief in me." John 16:9 Could this still be the church's greatest sin--**unbelief** in Jesus, (most will declare God without any trouble)? Remember we have two arch-enemies--our flesh and Satan. We are created with a body, a mind (soul) and a spirit. *The Spirit should rule and dominate our minds and bodies.* However, many times either our mind or our fleshly desires rule our spirit part. Clearly, we are going to need help if the good is to be in control! We will need assistance and reinforcement! That's where our powerful person of the Holy Spirit comes in.

Hopefully, we will learn from our study who He is as a person and appropriate His power. We certainly need all the help we can get in this present world, right?

HE IS THE ONLY PERSON OF THE TRINITY WHO IS NOW ON EARTH AND AVAILABLE TO US.

God the Father and Jesus Christ are not physically on this earth now, but the person of the Holy Spirit is. Therefore, *He is the only person of the Trinity on earth who is available to us.* However, Jesus is not limited by time or space and could reveal Himself or come to a person here on earth if he so chooses. But if we choose to *ignore, grieve, quench, insult and resist Him*, who else is available to help us? Who? Jesus gave us no one else. Scripture mentions no other Helper. Do we need help? Does the world offer any alternative plan? Let's look at our options. A wise person considers all his options. Satan came to kill, steal and destroy; so clearly he is not going to work for my good. Who else in all our world can be trusted but God the Father, Jesus His Son and the Holy Spirit?

Has there ever been any religion or cult that offered more than Jesus Christ? **WHAT OTHER LEADER PROVED HIS LOVE BY LAYING DOWN HIS LIFE VOLUNTARILY FOR ALL MEN (GOOD & BAD)? WHAT OTHER RELIGIOUS LEADER WAS RESURRECTED FROM THE DEAD AND IS STILL ALIVE TODAY TO HELP US?**

THE PERSON OF THE HOLY SPIRIT

Never make the mistake of having your god precede you in death.

Are not most of our problems of fear, anxiety, worry, grief, disappointment, depression deep within our own selves? Isn't that where the suffering takes place? So our spirit needs bolstering, strengthening, and calming. Satan's major weapon is deception. He appears as an angel of light but with a dagger concealed. Did Satan deceive Eve? Certainly or she wouldn't have eaten the apple. *Remember there is always some truth in deception*--that's why we are deceived because there is some truth mixed in. Isn't it interesting that most, if not all, cults use *some* Scripture in their doctrine?

Why do you think there has not been more awareness taught or more emphasis put on the person of the Holy Spirit?

It has been said that the spirituality of Christendom is at a far lower ebb today than it was 30 years ago. "Numbers of professing Christians have increased, fleshly activities have multiplied, but spiritual power has waned. Why? Because there is a grieved and quenched Spirit in our midst. While His blessing is withheld there can be no improvement. Until we recognize that we are entirely dependent upon His operations for all spiritual blessing, the root of the problem cannot be reached. Until it be recognized that it is 'Not by might (of trained workers), nor by power (of intellectual argument or persuasive appeal), but by MY SPIRIT, saith the Lord (Zech. 4:6), there will be no deliverance from that fleshly zeal which is not according to knowledge, and which is now paralyzing Christendom. Until the Holy Spirit is honored, sought, and counted upon, the present spiritual drought must continue." *The Holy Spirit* by Arthur W. Pink. page 9.

If Satan can keep you deceived about who the Holy Spirit really is, he has a captive in his camp. You are powerless to loose yourself. Remember Satan wanted to be God and was cast out of heaven, so he is an archenemy of God and is recruiting tirelessly for our eternal spirits. He hates all that is good, dislikes submission and authority. That's why he rebelled and was thrown out.

Is the spirit of the Lord a force or a Friend?

Is the Holy Spirit a power or a Person?

Very important that we know the difference if He is to become real to us. We need to begin to *know* Him as a person, and stop just learning *about* Him.

My very dear friend, Georgie Horner, for 30 years read and collected everything she could get her hands on concerning the Royal Family. She had all their photographs, books and articles written about them. Georgie knew all *about* them, but she never met or *knew* any of them or had any friendship with them personally. There's a big difference!

Surrendering to Him, His love, His will and His direction, will accomplish great results.

If the Holy Spirit is a *power,* we'll want to get hold of it. If the Holy Spirit is a *Divine Person,* we'll want Him to get hold of us.

THE PERSON OF THE HOLY SPIRIT

If the Holy Spirit is a *power,* we'll want it to accomplish our will and whim. If the Holy Spirit is a *Divine Person,* we'll want to surrender more to Him in awe and wonder.

If the Holy Spirit is a *power,* we'll be proud we have it and feel superior to those who do not. If the Holy Spirit is a *Divine Person,* we are humbled that in His great love the very Third Person of the Trinity has chosen to dwell within us.

It is absolutely futile to attempt to understand the work of the Holy Spirit without first *knowing* Him as a person; and second, we fail to take advantage of the marvelous friendship and fellowship of the Holy Spirit.

<u>Like Christ, the Person of the Holy Spirit is Eternal and Living.</u>

He doesn't have a body as you and I know it. However, He is not without form. *In one sense, we become His body when He lives within us.* God is a spirit and we must worship Him in spirit and in truth. We know the Holy Spirit is wholly God and that He is profoundly personal.

Chapter 4

THE WORK OF THE HOLY SPIRIT

R. A. Torrey said, "Before one can correctly understand the work of the Holy Spirit, he must first of all *know* the Spirit himself. A frequent source of error and fanaticism about the work of the Holy Spirit is the attempt to study and understand His work without first coming to *know* Him as a person." He is a divine person. Just as the Father (John 6:27; Eph. 4:6) and the Son (Heb. 1:8) are divine, so is the Holy Spirit (Acts 5:3,4).

Peter refers to the Holy Spirit in Acts 5:4 as "God." ". . . Why is it that you have conceived this deed in your heart? You have not lied to men, but to God."

Please know that both the Old and New Testaments recognize the Holy Spirit as God and Lord. We can never begin to give the Holy Spirit the place that belongs to Him until we see who He is. *But once we see who He is, we can begin to appreciate what He does.*

We need to realize that He is not merely an ambassador of the Almighty or an agent--He is a divine member of the Godhead. As Billy Graham said, "There is nothing that God is that the Holy Spirit is not. All of the essential aspects of deity belong to the Holy Spirit."

THE PERSON OF THE HOLY SPIRIT

How Do We Know the Spirit is a Person?

"When He, the Spirit of truth, has come, He will guide you into all truth...." John 16:13. The Holy Spirit has a unique personality--to think, to communicate, and to express His love; He is also easily grieved by our careless words and actions. *God's Spirit has all knowledge.* "For what man knows the things of a man except the spirit of the man which is in him? Even so no one knows the things of God except the Spirit of God." I Cor. 2:11.

The Holy Spirit Has a Mind:

"Likewise the Spirit also helps in our weaknesses. For we do not know what we should pray for as we ought, but the *Spirit Himself makes intercession for us with groanings which cannot be uttered.* Now He who searches the hearts knows what the mind of the Spirit is, (ideas of thought, feeling and purpose) because He makes intercession for the saints (Christians) *according to the will of God."*
Rom. 8:26,27.

". . .But strange as it seems, we Christians actually do have within us a portion of the very thoughts and mind of Christ." I Cor. 2:15.

Jesus said, "He will teach us all things, and bring to our remembrance all things that I said to you." John 14:26.

"But when the Helper comes, whom I shall send to you from the Father, the Spirit of truth who proceeds from the Father, He will testify of me." John 15:26.

The Holy Spirit is Our Guide.

"When the Holy Spirit, who is truth, comes, he shall **guide you into all truth,** for he will not be presenting his own ideas, but will be passing on to you what he has heard. *He will tell you about the future."* John 16:13.

The Holy Spirit is the Administrator of the Church.

When Christ returned to heaven, He placed the Holy Spirit in charge of the Church. Paul wrote, "The same Spirit works all these things, *distributing to each one individually as He wills."* I Cor. 12:11. Paul told the elders of the church at Ephesus, "The Holy Spirit has made you overseers." Acts 20:28. "He who has an ear, let him hear what the Spirit says to the churches." Rev. 2:7.

The Holy Spirit gives and sets all the gifts into their proper body parts so the body can function to its fullest ability to benefit the whole church. "For just as we have many members in one body and all the members do not have the same function, so we, who are many, are one body in Christ, and individually members one of another. And since we have gifts that differ according to the grace given to us, *let each exercise them accordingly. . ."* Romans 12:4-6. NAS.

Of course, Christ is the head of the body. "But speaking the truth in love, we are to grow up in all aspects into Him, who is the head, even Christ, from whom the whole body, being fitted and held together by that which every joint supplies, according to the *proper working* of each individual part, causes the growth of the body for the

THE PERSON OF THE HOLY SPIRIT

building up of itself in love." Eph. 4:15-16. NAS.

It is vital that we stay in tune with the direction of the Holy Spirit, or we could find ourselves on the wrong path. Have you ever made a major or minor decision without consulting the Holy Spirit, only to find yourself in deep trouble later?

Jesus Made a Promise!

Jesus told the disciples that His return to heaven was in their best interest. "Nevertheless I tell you the truth. It is to your advantage that I go away; for if I do not go away, the Helper will not come to you; but if I depart, I will send Him to you." John 16:7.

As long as Jesus Christ was here in the flesh, He was limited in this way: only a few could know Him, hear Him, and have fellowship with Him. He was limited by His earthly body. Jesus told them they couldn't bear all he could have taught them while on earth (John 16:12). "However, when He, the Spirit of truth, has come, *He will guide you into all truth;* for He will not speak on His own authority, but whatever He hears He will speak; and *He will tell you things to come.* He will glorify Me....John 16:13-15.

Jesus then said, "It is better for you that I go away. And I will pray the Father, and He will give you another Helper (a Comforter), that *He may abide with you forever."* John 14:16.

The Holy Spirit Speaks to the Inner Man.

The natural mind has great difficulty truly receiving the things of God. That is one of the reasons why the Lord often spoke in parables. Jesus knew that when the Holy Spirit made His entrance, the disciples would discover more about the Master than when He walked with them on earth. The Holy Spirit would reveal the Lord Jesus to their *hearts*.

The Holy Spirit is a Wonderful Communicator.

But He does not speak for the sake of passing along information. He speaks to get a response. *He waits for us to hear and eventually obey.*

We've Been Adopted!

"For you did not receive the spirit of bondage again to fear, but you received the Spirit of adoption by whom we cry out, "Abba, Father." Rom. 8:15. It is the Holy Spirit who makes it possible for *every believer to be welcomed into the family of God.*

The Holy Spirit Convicts and Convinces!

The Lord Jesus said that when the Holy Spirit comes "He will convict the world of sin, and of righteousness and of judgment." John 16:8.

Jesus tells us that we can never receive anything from Him without the Holy Spirit enabling us. John 16:14. What makes the Christian life so exciting? Because the Holy Spirit is always revealing something unique and original. It is certainly never dull or monotonous.

THE PERSON OF THE HOLY SPIRIT

For instance, I was impressed and compelled to start reading and researching on the person of the Holy Spirit. The urging became stronger and stronger and for what reason, I do not know at this writing. It has been richly rewarding to my spirit. Just have to obey--don't have to know why.

The Day the Spirit Came to Earth:

One hundred twenty of his followers gathered together in the Upper Room. Among them was Mary, mother of Jesus, the Lord Jesus' brothers, the apostles and others. For ten days they waited and prayed for the promise. "And suddenly there came a sound from heaven, as of a rushing mighty wind, and it filled the whole house where they were sitting." Acts 2:2. *The person of the Holy Spirit was sent to earth on God's timetable--not man's.*

Wind and Fire!

"Immediately there appeared what seemed to be tongues of fire that separated and sat upon each of them. And they were all filled with the Holy Spirit and began to speak with other tongues, as the Spirit gave them utterance." Acts 2:3,4. When they walked out of the Upper Room they *were transformed.* They began to declare the gospel with power--world-shaking power. *The Holy Spirit was His invisible Self present in the body of believers.*

As a result of the Lord Jesus going to the Father and sending the Holy Spirit, believers would be able to do greater works: Jesus said, **"In solemn truth I tell you,**

anyone believing in me shall do the same miracles I have done, and even greater ones, because I am going to be with the Father." John 14:12

Some of the religious leaders of Jesus' day accepted His ability to heal but rejected His ability to forgive sin. Today it's just the opposite; many believers who have no problem believing that Jesus forgives sin are absolutely resistant to the idea that He wants to heal people today.

Because of His sovereign choice to work through believers, God will not do it without *us,* and we cannot do it without *Him.*

We know that when the Holy Spirit arrives He announces His entry. But remember, He never announces His departure. For instance, Samson did not know that the Lord had departed from him. Judges 16:20. The Spirit of the Lord departed from Saul, and was replaced by an unclean spirit. I Sam. 16:14.

<u>The Holy Spirit Can Love.</u>

Love is more than a characteristic of the Holy Spirit, it is His character. *God so loved* us that He sent His Son. *His Son so loved* us that He died for us. And the *Holy Spirit so loved* us that He came and revealed the Lord Jesus to us, enabling us to become more and more like the Christ.

GOD IS LOVE--ALL LOVE; THEREFORE, LOVE IS A PERSON.

Left to our own devices, we would not be capable of loving

THE PERSON OF THE HOLY SPIRIT

God and desiring His companionship where we could say, "It's not so much the asking Jesus to make me this or that but the living with Him, thinking of Him, talking to Him-- thus grow like Him. Love Him. Rest in Him. Joy in Him." It's the Holy Spirit within us that creates the desire and capacity to love God and His Son more fully.

<u>The Holy Spirit Can Be Grieved.</u>

He is likened to a dove. Just as the Lord was grieved by the hardness of their hearts, (Mark 3:5) the Holy Spirit can also be grieved by our actions and our wrong attitudes. Being ignored is a grievous hurt. Paul was speaking to the Church, "Do not grieve the Holy Spirit of God, by whom you were sealed for the day of redemption." Eph. 4:30.

The word *grieve* means "torment, cause sorrow, vex, offend, insult or cause pain." The Holy Spirit has a tender heart that will easily weep for you and me. As we keep our hearts pure and just, and recognize and consult Him, we will not grieve Him.

If we have knowingly or unknowingly *offended* the Holy Spirit, we need to clear that up with Him right away. Just as we have to do with our friends with whom we have offended or had a falling out with. The relationship and friendship can not be restored until the *offense* is cleared up. This was true with a friend of mine. I had heard she said something about my husband which wasn't true. Later, she wanted to know why I was cool to her. I explained that I could be a casual friend but never an intimate friend until this matter was cleared up. It was two years later, she came and apologized to my husband. She explained that she had been given the wrong information and she was sorry. Our friendship and love was quickly restored. Pretending that the offense did not occur and going on as usual does not work. It's like a big old nasty carbunkle with a hard festering core that must be excised before it can be restored to health again.

The Holy Spirit not only speaks directly, He also chooses to speak *through* His people. David said, "The Spirit of the Lord spoke by me, and His word was on my tongue."
2 Sam. 23:2.

The voice of the Holy Spirit is not limited to special individuals or special occasions, like in Old Testament times.

He wants to speak to us today and every day. May we listen closely and hear His voice in every situation. Very often He speaks in a still small voice, intimating we have to be in close proximity to hear anything--like lovers.

The Holy Spirit Can Be Insulted.

When we fail to appreciate the significance of Christ's death on the cross for us, we *insult* the Holy Spirit. The word *insult* here carries with it the idea of "treating with utter contempt or arrogantly insulting."

"Think how much more terrible the punishment will be for those who have trampled underfoot the Son of God and treated his cleansing blood as though it were common and unhallowed, and insulted and outraged the Holy Spirit who brings God's mercy to his people." Heb. 10:29.

THE PERSON OF THE HOLY SPIRIT

Remember, the person of the Holy Spirit would have never been sent to the world on the day of Pentecost if Christ had not shed His blood, been resurrected and returned to the Father.

Why is insulting the Holy Spirit such a serious matter? It will result in losing His presence, removing His anointing and fellowship.

The Holy Spirit Can Be Lied To.

Ananias and Sapphira lied to the Holy Spirit and they were struck dead after sinning against God by lying to the Holy Spirit. Acts 5:5,9,10.

He Can Be Blasphemed.

"Every sin and blasphemy will be forgiven men, but the blasphemy against the Spirit will not be forgiven men. . . *either in this age or in the age to come."* Matt. 12:31,32.

Remember the Pharisees had just seen Jesus cast demons out of a demon-possessed man, healing him of blindness and muteness also. Matt. 12:22. "This fellow does not cast out demons except by Beelzebub, the ruler of the demons." Matt. 12:24. They were students of the Law, rulers of the people, and eyewitnesses to the miracles of the Lord Jesus.

THEY ATTRIBUTED THE MIRACLE OF CHRIST TO THE WORKING OF SATAN. THEY ATTRIBUTED THE POWER OF THE HOLY SPIRIT AT WORK IN THE LIFE OF JESUS TO THE INFILLING OF THE

EVIL ONE.

"He who blasphemes against the Holy Spirit, *never has forgiveness,* but is subject to eternal condemnation." Mark 3:29.

The *unpardonable* sin was willfully attributing to Satan the miracles performed by Christ through the power of the Holy Spirit.

Have you ever heard anyone or possibly a minister say, "Some of the gifts of the Holy Spirit are of the devil?" Very dangerous! You have a better chance if you are an unbeliever, but having studied and learned the Scriptures and making such statements is very serious! *When we don't know, should we not search the Scriptures, and then keep silent if we are not sure just what happened in some extreme or misuse of some gift?* God says that He will do the judging!

Have you noticed that many curse using the name of God and Jesus Christ, but never have I heard anyone curse using the name of the Holy Spirit. Isn't it ingenious that the Holy Spirit is invisible or man would try to kill Him like they did Jesus if they could get their hands on Him? In the Godhead, the Holy Spirit is the One we are warned not to quench, resist, grieve or offend.

<u>The Holy Spirit Can Be Resisted.</u>

Stephen, full of the Holy Spirit, stood before the Sanhedrin--the high court of the Jews--and said, "You stiff-necked and uncircumcised in heart and ears! *You always resist the Holy*

THE PERSON OF THE HOLY SPIRIT

Spirit; as your fathers did, so do you." Acts 7:51-55.

It is very dangerous to refuse to hearken to the words of the Holy Spirit, for there can come a point when He will ignore our words if we ignore His. "My Spirit shall not strive with man forever. . ." Gen. 6:3

"A man who remains stiff-necked after many rebukes will suddenly be destroyed--without remedy." Proverbs 29:1.

"There is no use trying to bring you back to the Lord again if you have once understood the Good News and tasted for yourself the good things of heaven and shared in the Holy Spirit, and know how good the Word of God is, and felt the mighty powers of the world to come, and then have turned against God. You cannot bring yourself to repent again if you have nailed the Son of God to the cross again by rejecting him, holding him up to mocking and to public shame." Heb. 6:4.

He Can Be Quenched.

Paul said in I Thes. 5:19,20, "Do not quench the Spirit; do not despise prophetic utterances." NAS.

The world resists the Holy Spirit, but BELIEVERS can actually QUENCH Him. The imagery used is that of putting out a fire. The word *quench* means: to *extinguish; put out; to overcome; subdue; suppress.* Paul was not talking to sinners, but to the *brethren.*

An unbeliever resists Him by rejecting the message of the gospel and refusing to allow the Holy Spirit to work in his life. *The child of God, however, QUENCHES a flame that has already started to burn.* There are some people who pray for some of the gifts of the Holy Spirit--but not all of them. They pull out their spiritual fire extinguisher and douse the flame.

WOULD YOU REFUSE ANY GIFT THAT THE HOLY SPIRIT OFFERED YOU? The Holy Spirit gives the gift or gifts as He chooses. We do not choose, but we can covet and earnestly contend for the best gifts.

How can we decide whether a spiritual phenomenon is from God or another source? It is by the fruit it produces, and sometimes that takes time.

William De Arteaga says that the greatest threat to a move of the Holy Spirit in our lives does not come from atheists or humanists. It comes from within the church. It's the same opposition Jesus faced. The Pharisees, who should have been the first to recognize the Messiah, instead became the first to attack Him. They rejected His theology because it differed from *their* traditions and customs.

Don't let anyone engage you in an argument or debate about how, when or where you receive the Holy Spirit. The important issue is to learn as much as you can about the person of the Holy Spirit and *He* will guide you into all truth. Earnestly seek to know Him personally, and believe what He wrote in Scripture.

THE PERSON OF THE HOLY SPIRIT

Chapter 5

THE ATTRIBUTES OF THE HOLY SPIRIT

The Holy Spirit is Omnipresent--Present Everywhere.

Where can I go from your Spirit?
Or where can I flee from your presence?
If I ascend into heaven, You are there.
If I make my bed in hell, behold, You are there.
If I take the wings of the morning,
And dwell in the uttermost parts of the sea,
Even there Your hand shall lead me,
And your right hand shall hold me.
Psa. 139:7-10.

The Holy Spirit is Omniscient--All Knowing.

It is very productive to ask a person who has all the facts and answers. "But the Comforter, which is the Holy Ghost, whom the Father will send in my name, he shall teach you all things, and bring all things to your remembrance, whatsoever I have said unto you." John 14:26 KJV

He is Omnipotent--All Powerful.

Creation; bringing life from non-life; resurrection--bringing life from death.

When I look at an electric light I realize that the source of that light is hidden from view. Somewhere there is a generator producing power. We don't always appreciate this, let alone understand it--but we enjoy the benefits. *The Holy Spirit is our generator for abundant life--hidden from view.* He is the source of the abundant life we enjoy. Nothing happens in our life without His power.

The more dependent and weak we are, the more He can show Himself strong on our behalf. This is a paradox! We have been taught just the opposite in the physical realm--if we exercise a lot the stronger we will become. In the spiritual realm, our strength comes from the Holy Spirit empowering us from *within.*

The Holy Spirit is Eternal.

He has always been, He is, and always will be. He is without beginning or end. The Holy Spirit did not suddenly come onto the scene when He was sent to earth to empower believers after the ascension of Christ. He's always the same and He will always be the same, and the eternal Holy Spirit will never let you down. He's the same yesterday, today, and forever!

"Only the Holy Spirit gives eternal life. Those born only once, with physical birth, will never receive this gift. But now I have told you how to get this true spiritual life. But some of you don't believe me...." John 6:63,64. TLB

"It is the Spirit who gives life; the flesh profits nothing; the words that I have spoken to you are spirit and are life. But there are some of you who do not believe...." John 6:63,64 NAS.

THE PERSON OF THE HOLY SPIRIT

The Holy Spirit is Immutable

"In the same way God, desiring even more to show to the heirs of the promise the unchangeableness of His purpose, interposed with an oath, in order that by two unchangeable things, in which it is impossible for God to lie, we may have strong encouragement, we who have fled for refuge in laying hold of the hope set before us." Heb.6:17,18. NAS

Chapter 6

NAMES OF THE HOLY SPIRIT

<u>The Spirit of God </u>(associated with power, prophecy, and guidance). Gen. 1:2; I Sam. 10:10; 2 Chron. 24:20; Ezek. 11:24; Matt. 12:28; Rom. 8:14; I Cor. 3:16.

<u>The Spirit of the Lord.</u> The Spirit of the "I AM." Judges 6:34, 7:2; Isa. 59:19; Luke 4:18; 2 Cor. 3:17.

"And if the Spirit of God, who raised up Jesus from the dead, lives in you, he will make your dying bodies live again after you die, by means of this same Holy Spirit living within you." Rom. 8:11.

<u>My Spirit.</u>

"And it will come about after this that I will pour out My Spirit on all mankind; and your sons and daughters will prophesy, your old men will dream dreams, your young men will see visions." Joel 2:28. "Then the Lord said, "My Spirit shall not strive with man forever, because he also is flesh; nevertheless his days shall be 120 years." Gen. 6:3. "Then he answered and said to me, "This is the word of the Lord to Zerubbabel saying, 'Not by might nor by power, but by My Spirit' says the Lord of hosts." Zech. 4:6.

<u>The Spirit of the Living God.</u>

"The Holy Spirit makes God's Word so real to us and in us,

THE PERSON OF THE HOLY SPIRIT

making His Word live and His children "living epistles." 2 Cor. 3:3. "You are a letter from Christ written not with ink but with the Spirit of the living God, not on tablets of stone but on tablets of human hearts. He has made us competent as ministers of a new covenant—not of the letter but of the Spirit; *for the letter kills, but the Spirit gives life."* 2 Cor. 3:1-6.

The Power of the Highest.

"The angel replied, "The Holy Spirit shall come upon you, and the power of God shall overshadow you; so the baby born to you will be utterly holy—the Son of God." Luke 1:35.

The Spirit of Christ.

Long before Jesus came, the prophets declared that His first coming would be as the *suffering Messiah,* and the second coming of Christ as the *conquering Messiah.* The Spirit of the Lord inspired the human authors of Scriptures. 2 Peter 1:21. "He will testify of Me." John 15:26. "The testimony of Jesus is the spirit of prophecy." Rev. 19:10.

The Spirit of Jesus Christ.

Paul said, "I know that this will turn out for my deliverance through your prayer and the supply of *the Spirit of Jesus Christ.* " Phil. 1:19. The Lord Jesus wanted our joy to be complete (John 16:24) and prayed for the Father to send another Helper to abide with us and make our joy complete. *Joy comes through the Spirit of Jesus Christ regardless of our condition.*

The Spirit of His Son.

"And because you are sons, God has sent forth the Spirit of His Son into your hearts, crying out, 'Abba, Father!' Therefore you are no longer a slave but a son, and if a son, then an heir of God through Christ." Gal. 4:6,7. *Abba* is the term in Aramaic that small children would use in addressing their father, like *Daddy,* or *Papa.* The term is polite, intimate, and tender.

The Spirit of Adoption.

The moment we believe on Christ as our Savior, something marvelous happens. We are adopted into God's family. Instantly, we are given power to become *children* of God. John 1:12. He called us to "adoption as sons by Jesus Christ to Himself, according to the good pleasure of His will." Eph. 1:5. We now have the rights, privileges and responsibilities that go with being a member of the family. Read Rom 8:23. When will our adoption be culminated? When our bodies are redeemed at the Rapture, or at the Second Coming of Christ.

"For his Holy Spirit speaks to us deep in our hearts, and tells us that we really are God's children....*But if we are to share his glory, we must also share his suffering."* Rom. 8:15.

The Spirit of Glory.

"If you are reproached for the name of Christ, blessed are you, for the Spirit of glory and of God rests upon you." 1

THE PERSON OF THE HOLY SPIRIT

Peter 4:14.

The Spirit of Grace.

Who do you suppose conveys this grace to us? The Holy Spirit. He ministers grace to us moment by moment. "...Of how much worse punishment, do you suppose, will he be thought worthy who has trampled the Son of God underfoot, counted the blood of the covenant by which he was sanctified a common thing, and **insulted** the Spirit of *grace?*" Heb. 10:28-29.

The Spirit of Wisdom and Understanding.

Wisdom is living with skill--it is the ability to apply the knowledge of God's Word in our daily life--and nothing less. Read all of Isaiah 11.

The Spirit of Counsel and Might.

Isaiah 9:6 describes the Holy Spirit as "The Spirit of counsel and might." The Lord Jesus said, "You shall receive power when the Holy Spirit has come upon you." Acts 1:8. Are we experiencing power and strength to overcome whatever bothers or troubles us?

The Spirit of Knowledge and the Fear of the Lord.

Also in Isaiah 11 refers to the knowledge and fear of the Lord. When we are in tune with the leading of the Holy Spirit, we gain a fuller understanding of the world around us, and every day can be a day of awe and wonder. He not only brings knowledge, the Holy Spirit also brings the *fear of the Lord.* Solomon said, "The fear of the Lord is the beginning of knowledge, but fools despise wisdom and instruction." Prov. 1:7.

Do we fear the devil more than we fear God? Fear God, and we won't need to fear the devil. "He who is in you is greater than he who is in the world." I John 4:4. Who brings this ability to fear and reverence the Lord? The Holy Spirit.

We should have more *faith in God* than we do in the *devil's ability to deceive us!*

The Spirit of Life.

"I have come that they may have life, and that they may have it more abundantly." John 10:10. Who ministers this abundant life to us? The Holy Spirit. "It is the Spirit who gives life; the flesh profits nothing. The words that I speak to you are spirit, and they are life." John 6:63. The Spirit of the Lord is waiting to heal your past, guarantee your future, and liberate you to experience abundant life right here and now. Dr. T. L. Osborn said, "We can have a future if we will give up the past."

The Holy Spirit of Promise.

Paul said that those who have trusted Christ as their Savior are "sealed with the Holy Spirit of promise, who is the guarantee of our inheritance." Eph. 1:13,14. The indwelling of the Holy Spirit within us is a promise that one day we will receive all that has been promised and prepared

THE PERSON OF THE HOLY SPIRIT

for us: *a new body, a new nature, and a new home.*

The Spirit of Truth.

The Holy Spirit has a specific assignment from God to communicate and impart what is true and valid. The Lord Jesus described Him as "the Spirit of truth, whom the world cannot receive, because it neither sees Him nor knows Him; but you know Him, for He dwells *with* you and will be *in* you." John 14:17. "When He, the Spirit of truth, has come, He will guide you into all truth. He will tell you about the future." John 16:13.

"But we know about these things because God has sent his Spirit to tell us, and his Spirit searches out and shows us all of God's deepest secrets. . . And no one can know God's thoughts except God's own Spirit." I Cor. 2:10-11.

"And the way to find out if their message is from the Holy Spirit is to ask: Does it really agree that Jesus Christ, God's Son, actually became man with a human body? If so, then the message is from God." I John 4:2.

The Comforter.

"I will pray the Father, and He shall give you another Comforter, that he may abide with you forever." John 14:16. Comforter in Greek is Paraclete--meaning *one called alongside to help.* A defense attorney, and an advocate, a helper who will fight your battles, a helper who is so good at what He does that He calms our restless fear.

The Eternal Spirit.

"...how much more shall the blood of Christ, who through the eternal Spirit offered Himself without spot to God, purge your conscience from dead works to serve the living God?" Heb. 9:14.

The Spirit.

He is often referred to in Scripture simply as *the Spirit*. Read John 1:32; John 3:5. Again and again we are encouraged to *be filled with the Spirit*. Acts 9:17; Eph. 5:18. He is the Spirit of the Father and the Son. Are we ready to invite the Holy Spirit into our lives? He will be our Counselor, our Helper, our Teacher and Guide.

Holy Spirit Speaking the Word.

The Father, the Son, and the Holy Spirit were all present at creation. The Father is the Source (John 5:26), the Son is the Channel of that Source (Acts 2:22), and the Holy Spirit is the Power that flows through that Channel (Acts 1:8; 2:33). He releases the Source and touches our life.

"For no prophecy recorded in Scripture was ever thought up by the prophet himself. It was the Holy Spirit within these godly men who gave them true messages from God." 2 Peter 1:20,21.

The strong, yet quiet Spirit of God was totally involved in everything the Father designed--from a glittering star to a raging storm. The Word contained the authority of the entire Godhead. "In the beginning was the Word, and the Word was with God, and the Word was God. He was in

THE PERSON OF THE HOLY SPIRIT

the beginning with God. All things were made through Him, and without Him nothing was made that was made." John 1:1-3. Read Heb. 1:2.

Chapter 7

HOLY SPIRIT CARRIES THE VOICE OF THE FATHER

Breath of Life.

Just as your breath carries your voice, so the Holy Spirit carries the voice of the Father. Read 1 Cor. 2:6-16. J. Rodman Williams, a noted Bible scholar says, "The Breath that God breathes into man's nostrils is more than physical breath (though it is that, too). It is also spiritual breath because God is spirit." "The Spirit of God has made me, and the breath of the Almighty gives me life." Job 33:4.

"And when He had said this, He breathed on them, and said to them, 'Receive the Holy Spirit.'" Isa. 42:5, "Thus says God the Lord, Who created the heavens and stretched them out, Who spread out the earth and its offspring, Who gives breath to the people on it, and spirit to those who walk in it,. . . " He is also the one who "forms the spirit of man within him." Zech. 12:1.

"God's ways are as mysterious as the pathway of the wind, and as the manner in which a human spirit is infused into the little body of a baby *while it is yet in its mother's womb.*" Ecc. 11:5

The Holy Spirit Sustains Life.

The Holy Spirit has been given an awesome task: to create,

THE PERSON OF THE HOLY SPIRIT

maintain, and renew--in both our physical body and the material world. The writer of Hebrews tells us that the Son's task also includes "upholding all things by the word of His power." Heb. 1:3.

When the Holy Spirit arrives, things are restored and refreshed. The Psalmist said, "You send forth Your Spirit, they are created; And You renew the face of the earth." Psa. 104:30.

Why are we breathing? Why are we alive? It is because the Spirit of God has placed breath in my nostrils. Job 27:3. He's enabling me to live. Not only spiritually, but He is the source of my physical being. "...but if by the Spirit you put to death the deeds of the body, you will live. For as many as are led by the Spirit of God, these are the *sons* of God." Rom 8:6,13,14.

"The Spirit of God has made me, and the breath of the Almighty gives me life." Job 33:4. "Gives me life"--that is, moment-by-moment, day-by-day He sustains and gives life. That's one reason it's so important to have a vital relationship with the Holy Spirit. Life apart from Him is no life--real life--at all.

The Holy Spirit Imparts Order.

Moses led the Children of Israel by an orderly plan. It was precise and specific. Jesus had the people seated in groups of 50 and 100 when he fed the 5,000. We are further instructed by Paul that all things are to be done decently and in order in the church.

Even though we make our plans, we must never attempt to organize the Holy Spirit. He must be allowed to do His perfect will. Always flow with His plans and never expect Him to flow with ours. *We always prepare, but we do not allow our preparations to come before His plans.* In I Cor. 12 He is the *Spirit of power.* In chapter 13 He is the *Spirit of love.* In chapter 14 He is the *Spirit of order.* Where there is love and power, there is order.

When the Holy Spirit Transforms Us, He Will Turn Our Wilderness Into a Fruitful Place.

"The Spirit will be poured upon us from on high, and the wilderness becomes a fruitful field, and the fruitful field is counted as a forest." Isa. 32:15. "By this My Father is glorified, that you bear much fruit." John 15:8. It's not our fruit, but His. That's why the Scripture calls it the *fruit of the Spirit.*

He Will Cause Us to Walk with God.

"I will put my Spirit within you and cause you to walk in My statutes, and you will keep My judgments and do them." Ezek. 36:27.

A new Christian looks at the laws of God and says, "It is not possible to keep those rules and regulations!" They are right. Howard Hendricks said, "The Christian life isn't difficult--it's impossible!" In our own power we will fail, but the Holy Spirit causes us to walk in God's ways. *Remember, without the Holy Spirit within us we cannot walk with God. It is the Holy Spirit's power that is able to keep us from stumbling,* and to present us faultless before

THE PERSON OF THE HOLY SPIRIT

the presence of His glory with exceeding joy. Jude 1:24.

". . .We do not tell them that they must obey every law of God or die; but we tell them there is life for them from the Holy Spirit. The old way, trying to be saved by keeping the Ten Commandments, ends in death; in the new way, the Holy Spirit gives them life." 2 Cor. 3:6.

We can own and have the most recent powerful computer made, but until it is plugged into the power source, it is useless, even antagonistic! We can own the latest Lexus, but without *fuel* we aren't going any place. We are only a beautiful showpiece!

<u>We Will Know God's Presence.</u>

The Holy Spirit causes the presence of the Father to be a reality in our lives, and as a result of this we feel His closeness. "And when you draw close to God, God will draw close to you. . ." James 4:8. Notice, the first move is ours! Make an intentional effort to spend time in the presence of the Lord. Talk with Him, love Him, acknowledge Him, get up close to Him!

". . . the Holy Spirit warns us to listen to him, to be careful to hear his voice today and not let our hearts become set against him, as the people of Israel did. They steeled themselves against his love and complained against him in the desert while he was testing them." Heb. 3:7-8.

<u>We Will Understand God's Word.</u>

"Surely I will pour out my spirit on you; I will make my

words known to you." Prov. 1:23. If we want the Bible to come alive, invite the Holy Spirit to read along with us. The same Holy Spirit that rested on the Lord Jesus is indwelling us. Being acquainted with Scripture simply isn't enough--the person of the Holy Spirit wants to be certain that the Word of God *abides* in you (I John 2:14).

We Will become a New Person.

He changes us from the *inside out*. It is total. "Therefore, if anyone is in Christ, he is a new creation; old things have passed away; behold, all things have become new." 2 Cor. 5:17. "I will give you a *new heart* and put a *new spirit* within you; I will take the heart of stone out of your flesh and give you an heart of flesh." Ezek. 36:26. Have we experienced this transformation?

He Will Give Us Rest.

The Spirit of the Lord doesn't lead us into stress or confusion. He gives us peace and calm. "In quietness and confidence shall be your strength." Isa. 30:15. The key to relief is not a prescription, a cruise, or learning, but spending time with the Holy Spirit to be rested and refreshed.

THE PERSON OF THE HOLY SPIRIT

Chapter 8

HOLY SPIRIT GIVES HOPE & COMFORT

<u>He Will Bring Excellence Into Our Life.</u>

He is the author of quality and perfection. "Daniel distinguished himself above the governors and satraps, because an excellent spirit was in him; and the king gave thought to setting him over the whole realm." Dan. 6:3. He had a surpassing spirit. We often advance or decline on the merit of our performance. Remember what happened in the life of Joseph? Pharaoh recognized the Holy Spirit in his life and he was made Prime Minister (Gen. 41:38).

Every day we need to allow the Spirit of the Lord to bring quality and distinction to our Christian walk.

<u>The Spirit Imparts the Character of God.</u>

The Holy Spirit doesn't merely reform us, He transforms our character into the character of God. "But we Christians have no veil over our faces; we can be mirrors that brightly reflect the glory of the Lord. And as the Spirit of the Lord works within us, we become more and more like him." 2 Cor. 3:18.

<u>The Spirit Strengthens the Inner Man.</u>

Man's measuring stick has always been the outward appearance, but the Lord looks on the heart. <u>IT ALL</u>

GLORY CHAPMAN

HAPPENS IN THE HEART!

His body-building program is designed to strengthen the inside of a man or woman. As the Holy Spirit begins to work in the depths of our soul, He strengthens us spiritually with spiritual strength and maturity that gives us an even greater level of faith and enables us to trust God for the impossible and believe Him for the invisible. No matter what the circumstance, no matter what challenge we may face, we will say with the Psalmist: "The Lord is my light and my salvation; Whom shall I fear? The Lord is the strength of my life; Of whom shall I be afraid?" Psa. 27:1. <u>Strength comes from deep within us as the Holy Spirit brings fearless, and sometimes even violent or combat faith to our life.</u>

We don't have to be strong. We only have to be in the company of the Holy Spirit, and we say in any difficult situation, "We are with Him."

The Spirit Liberates Us.

"Now the Lord is the Spirit; and where the Spirit of the Lord is, there is liberty." 2 Cor. 3:17. We've been liberated by the Holy Spirit from sin and for service. Isn't it grand that heaven is going to be filled with imperfect people who have been made perfect in God's sight by the work of Christ at Calvary? This mighty work is available to us through His Spirit.

The Spirit Brings Renewal.

In the book, *The Day America Told the Truth,* the authors

THE PERSON OF THE HOLY SPIRIT

ask Americans what they would most want to change about themselves in order to fulfill their potential as humans. How would we answer that question? Most of *them* answered: "They wanted to be rich and thin."

Who is the source of our renewal? "It is not by works of righteousness which we have done, but according to His mercy He saved us, through the washing of regeneration and renewing of the Holy Spirit." Titus 3:5.

Renewal does not mean to turn back the clock, it means a new you! A new quality of life. "...Reject profane and old wives' fables, and exercise yourself toward godliness. For bodily exercise profits a little, but godliness is profitable for all things, having promise of the life that now is and of that which is to come." I Tim. 4:7,8.

The Spirit Brings Us Hope.

Hope is looking forward to something with confidence or expectation. *Hope* is based on love, that is, that the One who loves us will do what He promised because of His love, and the Bible says that the *Holy Spirit gives hope when we are going through difficulties.*

"We can rejoice, too, when we run into problems and trials for we know that they are good for us--they help us learn to be patient. And patience develops strength of character in us and helps us trust God more each time we use it until finally our hope and faith are strong and steady. Then when that happens, we are able to hold our heads high no matter what happens and know that all is well, for we know how dearly God loves us, and we feel his warm love everywhere within us because God has given us the Holy Spirit to fill our hearts with his love." Rom. 5:3-5.

"Now may the *God of hope* fill you with all joy and peace in believing, that you may abound in *hope* by the power of the Holy Spirit." Rom. 15:13.

"He not only gives *hope* in the midst of the difficulties of the present, He also gives us *hope* for the joys of the future: For we through the Spirit eagerly wait for the *hope* of righteousness by faith." Gal. 5:5.

We can't live without hope. When depression and despair sets in, then suicide soon follows. We can live 40 days without food, a few days without water, a few minutes without oxygen, but only a short time without hope.

"Do you yearn for a new body and a new nature? It is our blessed hope--the glorious appearing of our great God and Savior, Jesus Christ." Titus 2:13. *Who is the source of this hope? It is the Holy Spirit who lives within us, pointing us to the return of Jesus Christ.*

The Holy Spirit Gives Comfort.

The Holy Spirit dwells within us, counseling, helping, comforting, taking up our cause when we need His help. Jesus meant that the coming Holy Spirit would be just like Himself. He will do in my absence what I would do if I were physically present with you. Those early believers endured times of persecution, walking "in the fear of the Lord and in the comfort of the Holy Spirit, and they were greatly multiplied." Acts 9:31.

THE PERSON OF THE HOLY SPIRIT

<u>The Spirit Gives Us Assurance.</u>

None of us come from perfect homes, and none of us provide perfect homes, no matter how hard we try. Perhaps your childhood was full of abuse, lack of love, insecurity, or turmoil. And beneath the anger or even the denial are deep feelings of hurt and profound questions about your worth or lovability as a person. When we trust Christ, the Holy Spirit transforms us from strangers into God's children, adopting us into God's wonderful family. *You become a member in the best family there is.*

One of the great works of the Spirit is that He "bears witness with our spirit that we are children of God." Rom. 8:16. **All inferiority, the sense of not belonging, the anger--can all be gone, replaced by the gentle voice of the Holy Spirit saying, "It's behind me now, the Father loves me and I am in His family now."**

And this happens at the level of our spirit. It is like a legal document as in an adoption. The Holy Spirit is a witness to our adoption and will vouch for us. He says, "Yes, I was there when you trusted Christ. Yes, you have been adopted into God's family, I witnessed it. Yes, you are a full member of the family. Yes, God is your loving heavenly Father. No, you don't need to be insecure about your new family."

<u>The Spirit's Presence is the Seal of Ownership and is Protected By the Owner.</u>

"And because of what Christ did, all you others too, who heard the Good News about how to be saved, and trusted

Christ, were marked as belonging to Christ by the Holy Spirit, who long ago had been promised to all of us Christians. His presence within us is God's guarantee that he really will give us all that he promised; and the Spirit's seal upon us means that God has already purchased us and that he guarantees to bring us to himself. This is just one more reason for us to praise our glorious God." Eph. 1:13,14.

Where is the Holy Spirit's Home?

"Haven't you yet learned that your body is the home of the Holy Spirit God gave you, and that he lives *within* you? Your own body does not belong to you. For God has bought you with a great price. So use every part of your body to give glory back to God, because he owns it." I Cor. 6:19.20.

THE PERSON OF THE HOLY SPIRIT

Chapter 9

BRINGS US INTO GOD'S PRESENCE

<u>The Holy Spirit Reveals the Things of God.</u>

The Holy Spirit delights to make things known to us that transcend our own thinking. You see, "no one knows the things of God except the Spirit of God." 1 Cor. 2:11. He is the author of the Bible; therefore, can reveal to us the things about God.

"Those who refuse to *plug in* to the Source of spiritual wisdom will never understand what the Lord has imparted to us, regardless of how studiously we study or how diligently we investigate. What will always set us apart is that *we have the mind of Christ."* I Cor. 2:16.

<u>The Holy Spirit Brings the Works of Christ to Our Remembrance.</u>

"He will teach you all things, and bring to your remembrance all things that I said to you." John 14:26. *Regardless of how much we may prepare a message,*the *Lord also has things He wants to communicate.* We need to be very sensitive to that. We can rely on the Holy Spirit as we study and as we deliver what the Holy Spirit has led us to prepare.

<u>The Holy Spirit Teaches Truth.</u>

"We are of God. He who knows God hears us; he who is not of God does not hear us. By this we know the spirit of truth and the spirit of error." 1 John 4:6.

There is a recently published book that is well disguised. It has many marvelous stories of individuals who have had an after-death experiences, came back to life, and have shared their glimpses of eternity. It includes well disguised reincarnation. Thank God that the Holy Spirit will alert us when something is in error. It is a New Age book! Remember our companion, the Holy Spirit, will expose error.

The Holy Spirit Causes Us to Be Occupied With Spiritual Things.

The miracle starts in the thought life. "For they that are after the flesh do mind the things of the flesh; but they that are after the Spirit the things of the Spirit. For to be carnally minded is death; but to be spiritually minded is life and peace." Rom. 8:5,6. KJV. Are we experiencing a shortage of peace?

"Men-made preachers and religionists may work night and day, to change flesh into spirit, they may toil from the cradle to the grave to fit people for Heaven, but after all their labors to wash the Ethiopian white and to rub the spots out of the leopard, flesh is flesh still and cannot by any possibility enter the kingdom of God. Nothing but the supernatural operations of the Holy Spirit will avail. Not only is man polluted to the very core by sin original and actual, but there is in him an absolute incapability to understand, embrace or enjoy spiritual things." A.W.Pink .

THE PERSON OF THE HOLY SPIRIT

"But the man who isn't a Christian can't understand and can't accept these thoughts from God, which the Holy Spirit teaches us. They sound foolish to him, because only those who have the Holy Spirit within them can understand what the Holy Spirit means. Others just can't take it in." I Cor. 2:14

The Holy Spirit Leads and Guides us.

"For as many as are led by the Spirit of God, these are *sons of God.*" Rom. 8:14.

"I advise you to obey only the Holy Spirit's instructions. *He will tell you where to go and what to do,* and then you won't always be doing the wrong things your evil nature wants you to. For we naturally love to do evil things that are just the opposite from the things that the Holy Spirit tells us to do...These two forces within us are constantly fighting each other to win control over us..." Gal. 5:16,17.

There is a black and white dog fighting within each of us. Guess which one wins? **THE ONE I FEED!**

The Holy Spirit Bears Witness of the Lord Jesus.

"Any work that exalts the Holy Spirit or the gifts above Jesus will finally land up in fanaticism. The Holy Spirit is a great light, but focused on Jesus always, for His revealing," says Frank Bartleman. In every great Christian, the focus has been upon the centrality of the Lord Jesus. "When the helper comes...He will testify of Me." John 15:26. The Apostle Paul said , ". . .no one speaking by the power of the Spirit of God can curse Jesus, and no one

can say, "Jesus is Lord," and really mean it, unless the Holy Spirit is helping him." I Cor. 12:3.

The Holy Spirit Opens Heaven.

Every time we welcome or invite the Holy Spirit in, He opens the portals of heaven and ushers us into the presence of our Father.

The Holy Spirit Brings Us Into God's Presence.

It's amazing how our perspective changes when the Lord is near. Mountains become foothills. Tears become smiles. Moses was able to endure the wilderness because God told him, "My *presence* will go with you, and I will give you rest." Ex. 33:14. We can say, with David, "In Your *presence* is fullness of joy." Psa. 16:11.

David pleaded, "Don't toss me aside, banished forever from your presence. Don't take your Holy Spirit from me. Restore to me again the joy of your salvation, and make me willing to obey you." Psa. 51:11,12.

No other religion known to man has ever claimed *God's presence* dwelt *within* man. In the Old Testament, God's glory and presence resided in the Tabernacle in the wilderness, then in Solomon's Temple and later in Zerubbabel's Temple.

After Christ was resurrected and ascended to the Father, He sent the marvelous gift of the Holy Spirit to reside *within the hearts of believers*. Awesome to think about!

THE PERSON OF THE HOLY SPIRIT

God's Dwelling Place- The Fourth Temple

In the beginning God dwelled in the Garden with man,
until the serpent came with guile to lead man astray.
Adam and Eve were expelled to live and labor on the land,
and man began to suffer from his sinful way.

God could no longer dwell in a place of such sinful shame,
but longed to fellowship with the man He created.
God then chose Abraham from whom nations came,
and to the chosen people of Israel's race He related.

"Build me a tabernacle," was God's earnest request,
so I'll have a dwelling place with the people I seek.
In the tabernacle above the Ark, I AM will rest,
a cloud would form there and from there I AM will speak.

Moses obeyed, and God traveled with them, a cloud by day.
And so it was, the tabernacle tent was God's dwelling place,
until Solomon finished the temple where the Ark would stay,
and there seal Israel's children as God's chosen race.

But Israel too often failed to honor the God of creation,
and fell into the worship of false gods and decadent sin;
bringing upon themselves God's judgment and damnation.
Would God's chosen people ever worship Him again?

So evil were they living in neglect of God's ways,
that God brought other nations, the temple to destroy.
Breaking it down from its former glory-filled days;
then to rebuild it, God's people, He would again employ.

Then sin invaded and the temple was doomed once more,
as the sin cycle continued and the temple was destroyed again.
Only to be rebuilt by Herod, with greater splendor than before,
to be visited by the Lamb of God, who lived without sin's stain.

GLORY CHAPMAN

This Jesus, God's only Son, became the sacrifice for all mankind. God, thereby building His fourth temple in the hearts of men. Never again has God's temple been difficult to find, for all who accept this Jesus, God comes to dwell within.

"Don't you know that you yourselves are God's temple and that God's Spirit lives in you? If anyone destroys God's temple, God will destroy him; for God's temple is sacred, and you are that temple." I Cor. 3:16 NIV

Emmitt J. Nelson
1996

THE PERSON OF THE HOLY SPIRIT

CHAPTER 10

HOLY SPIRIT HELPS IN PRAYER AND INTERCESSION

<u>The Holy Spirit Helps Us in Prayer and Intercession.</u>

He helps us when we pray, and He helps us by praying for us. It's called praying "in the Spirit." Jude 20 commands, "But you, dear friends, must build up your lives ever more strongly upon the foundation of our holy faith, learning to pray in the power and strength of the Holy Spirit."

Paul said , "Pray all the time. Ask God for anything in line with the Holy Spirit's wishes. Plead with him, reminding him of your needs, and keep praying earnestly for all Christians everywhere." Eph. 6:18

"The Spirit also helps in our weaknesses. For we do not know what we should pray for as we ought, but the Spirit Himself makes intercession for us with groanings which cannot be uttered." Rom. 8:26. The third Person of the Trinity, very God Himself, is intervening on our behalf. Don't let any circumstance, no matter how distressing, keep us from prayer. The Holy Spirit is waiting to plead your case before the Father. Wow!

<u>The Holy Spirit Intercedes With Groanings Which Cannot Be Uttered.</u>

The Holy Spirit takes our tangled thoughts and emotions, what we're praying for and what we *should* pray for, and brings it right to the Throne. If we ignore the part played by the Holy Spirit, we fail to use the right key.

The Holy Spirit Inspires Us to Worship.

When God's Spirit touches our spirit--that's worship!

In true worship, we meet the Lord with our spirits, intellect, will, and emotion. That's the difference between a cold, dead service and one that is vibrant and alive with God's presence.

Worship isn't singing about the Lord and praying that God will meet our needs; worship is lifting our praise to the Lord in love, devotion and adoration. Jesus said, "God is Spirit, and they that worship Him must worship him in spirit and in truth." John 4:24. KJV.

"Jesus replied, ". . .For it's not *where* we worship that counts, but *how* we worship--is our worship spiritual and real? Do we have the Holy Spirit's help? For God is Spirit, and we must have his help to worship as we should." John 4:22,23.

Who gives us the ability to really worship? The Holy Spirit. It is the Holy Spirit who reveals Jesus to us, and gives us the inner hunger and appetite for spiritual things.

The Holy Spirit Leads Us to Give Thanks.

Scripture tells us to "Talk with each other much about the Lord, quoting psalms and hymns and singing sacred songs, making music in your hearts to the Lord. Always give

THE PERSON OF THE HOLY SPIRIT

thanks *for everything* to our God and Father in the name of our Lord Jesus Christ." Eph. 5:19,20.

Being controlled by the Holy Spirit results in His anointing our speaking, our singing, our relationships and our perspective (giving thanks always for all things). It is so natural to be thankful only for the things that seem good at the time. But when the Holy Spirit has control, we'll be able to give thanks all the time, and for everything that comes our way--even the things that are not pleasant. "In *everything* give thanks; for this is the will of God in Christ Jesus for you." 1 Thess. 5:18.

When we can't think of anything to be thankful for, we can begin with our head, hair, eyes, ears, nose, mouth, teeth, brain, neck, arms, elbows, hands, chest, stomach, heart, all our organs, legs, ankles, feet and toes. By the end of that list, we should be joyfully thankful and say many "Thank-yous."

Chapter 11

FRUITS OF THE HOLY SPIRIT

<u>Remember, the Holy Spirit Is Not to Be the Object of Our Praise and Worship.</u>

Instead, we are instructed to recognize the Father and the Son as the source of all good things. But we thank them *through* the Holy Spirit. The Holy Spirit always focuses on Jesus Christ.

<u>The Holy Spirit Gives Us Power For Service.</u>

If God could use Moses who was a murderer, David who was an adulterer and murderer, and Paul who was a Pharisee and persecutor of Christians, then He can use us in some capacity to reach our world. We need to find our place in the family or body of Christ. If you haven't discovered where you belong, ask the Holy Spirit to help you. It is very important to know where to serve. It's a poor soldier who doesn't know where to serve and doesn't know who the enemy is.

Paul prayed for believers to accept the fact that they would "be strengthened with might through His Spirit." Eph. 3:16. He enables us to be more than we are capable of because we are not operating under our own steam.

<u>The Holy Spirit Performs Miracles Through Us.</u>

THE PERSON OF THE HOLY SPIRIT

We know that Jesus performed many miracles, yet He said of those who believe in Him: "In solemn truth I tell you, **anyone** believing in me shall do the same miracles I have done, and even greater ones, because I am going to be with the Father." John 14:12.

"God also bearing witness with them, both by signs and wonders and by various miracles and by gifts of the Holy Spirit according to His own will." Heb. 2:4. NAS

Billy Graham said that "as we approach the end of the age I believe we will see a dramatic recurrence of signs and wonders which will demonstrate the power of God to a skeptical world."

There is Joy, Peace and Righteousness in the Holy Spirit.

"For the kingdom of God is not meat and drink; but righteousness, and peace, and joy in the Holy Ghost." Rom. 14:17 KJV.

It's one thing to have peace and joy when everything is going our way. It's another thing altogether to maintain our peace and joy when the bottom falls out. It's one thing to love your children; it's another thing to love our enemy. Consequently, when the environment changes, the fruit withers and dies--and it is usually a quick death.

The most striking characteristic of men or women who are doing God's work His way is their lack of stress. Believers who are walking in the Spirit are going to experience peace.

The peace and joy experienced by an unregenerate man is the fruit of peaceful circumstances. Once the circumstances change, the same man may exhibit a violent temper. So the fruit of the Spirit demonstrates its divine source when circumstances and relationships take a turn for the worse. The reason is, the fruit of the Spirit is just that: fruit produced by the Spirit. It is not fragile. Its root is deeply embedded.

"And the disciples were continually filled with joy and with the Holy Spirit." Acts 13:52 NAS. This is a miracle since the Jewish leaders incited a mob against Paul and Barnabas, and ran them out of town. But they shook the dust of their feet against the town and went on to the city of Iconium. Remember joy does not depend upon circumstances, but upon a Person transfusing them in their invisible spirit part!

One of my favorite verses is, "The Lord himself is my inheritance, my prize. He is my food and drink, *my highest joy!* He guards all that is mine. He sees that I am given pleasant brooks and meadows as my share! What a wonderful inheritance! I will bless the Lord who counsels me; he gives me wisdom in the night. *He tells me what to do.*" Psa. 16:5-7.

<u>The Holy Spirit Liberates Us to Love.</u>

One of the first signs that God's Spirit is at work in our life is that we will have a great love for people--Christians and non-believers.

Dean Alford says, "This love is emphatically a gift, and in its full reference the *chief fruit of the Spirit."* Gal. 5:22; "It

THE PERSON OF THE HOLY SPIRIT

is this love of the Holy Spirit that empowers us to intercede for others, one of the greatest expressions of love we can have." Rom. 15:30.

"If I had the gift of being able to speak in other languages without learning them..., but didn't love others, I would only be making noise. If I had the gift of prophecy and knew all about what is going to happen in the future, knew everything about everything, but didn't love others, what good would it do? Even if I had the gift of faith so that I could speak to a mountain and make it move, I would still be worth nothing at all without love. If I gave everything I have to poor people, and if I were burned alive for preaching the Gospel but didn't love others, it would be of no value whatever." I Cor. 13:1-3.

"By this all men will know that you are My disciples, if you have *love for one another."* John 13:35. NAS.

The Holy Spirit Produces the Good Harvest and Fruit in Us.

The law of sowing and reaping is a well-established divine principle. What we plant determines what we will harvest-- whether it is good seed or bad. How do we *sow* to the Spirit? We rely on His power to reckon ourselves dead to the works of the flesh.

"But when you follow your own wrong inclinations your lives will produce these evil results: impure thoughts, eagerness for lustful pleasure, idolatry, spiritism (that is, encouraging the activity of demons), hatred and fighting, jealousy and anger, constant effort to get the best for yourself, complaints and criticisms, *the feeling that everyone else is wrong except those in your own little group*--and there will be wrong doctrine, envy, murder, drunkenness, wild parties, and all that sort of thing. Let me tell you again as I have before, that anyone living that sort of life will not inherit the kingdom of God." Gal. 5:19-21.

"But I say, walk by the Spirit, and you will not carry out the desire of the flesh." Gal. 5:16. NAS. The Spirit-filled life is not a life of DON'TS, it is a life of DO'S. Do walk in the Spirit, and you will avoid fulfilling your sinful desires. *Every sinful act is committed twice: once in our heads and once in our behavior.* First, we must win the battle that takes place in our minds. We have control over what we think!

"My true disciples produce bountiful harvests. This brings great glory to my Father." John 15:8.

How Do We Bear Fruit?

Jesus said, "Abide in Me, and I in you. As the branch cannot bear fruit of itself, unless it abides in the vine, neither can you, unless you abide in Me." John 15:4. He added, "I am the vine, you are the branches. He who abides in Me, and I in him, bears much fruit; for without Me you can do nothing." John 15:5.

It's the vine that does the work. The fruit is a product of the sap that flows from the vine into the branch. The Holy Spirit is the sap that runs from the vine into the branch. All

THE PERSON OF THE HOLY SPIRIT

we have to do is to keep *hanging on the vine and stay connected.* The fruit does not struggle to grow, but the Holy Spirit has begun to live and flow through us, producing the fruit of the Spirit. Apart from Him, we can do nothing, much less bear fruit. Hopefully, we will have regular harvests--not up one year and down the next. Try bearing fruit in your marriage without the Holy Spirit. It can't be done. Cut off the flow of the sap to the branch, and it slowly withers and dies—just as the physical body dies without nourishment. Make no mistake about it, we need help in all areas of our life. No problem, the Holy Spirit is certainly close by; in fact, He is *inside* us, waiting to be recognized and called upon. (Get the vacuum out and plug it into the power source).

The Sign of a Spirit-Filled Believer is Fruit, Not a Particular Experience.

God's plan of salvation includes a provision for saving us from ourselves. And the key player in that part of His plan is the Holy Spirit. He has provided us with every Person and provision possible so none would be lost to Him in eternity. What keeps us from running straight away to Him and sticking to Him like glue--like a child clings to his mother? What hinders you and me?

"BUT WHEN THE HOLY SPIRIT CONTROLS OUR LIVES HE WILL PRODUCE THIS KIND OF FRUIT IN US." Gal. 5:22-23. There are nine fruits:

LOVE   FOR THOSE WHO DO NOT LOVE IN

GLORY CHAPMAN

	RETURN.
<u>JOY</u>	IN THE MIDST OF PAINFUL CIRCUMSTANCES.
<u>PEACE</u>	WHEN SOMETHING YOU WERE COUNTING ON DOESN'T COME THROUGH.
<u>PATIENCE</u>	WHEN THINGS AREN'T GOING FAST ENOUGH FOR YOU.
<u>KINDNESS</u>	TOWARD THOSE WHO TREAT YOU UNKINDLY.
<u>GOODNESS</u>	TOWARD THOSE WHO HAVE BEEN INTENTIONALLY INSENSITIVE TO YOU.
<u>FAITHFULNESS</u>	WHEN FRIENDS HAVE PROVED UNFAITHFUL.
<u>GENTLENESS</u>	TOWARD THOSE WHO HAVE HANDLED YOU ROUGHLY.
<u>SELF-CONTROL</u>	IN THE MIDST OF INTENSE TEMPTATION.

Charles Stanley

The first three describe our *relationship to God,* the next three *our relationship to others,* and the final three *our inner self. The Holy Spirit is the only source for all of the fruit.*

THE PERSON OF THE HOLY SPIRIT

". . . for the joy of the Lord is your strength. . ." Neh. 8:10 There are many Scriptures about joy, peace, rest, and love! He wants us to be the happiest, most rested, loving, faithful, gentle, good and kind people on the face of the earth, and the Holy Spirit was sent to do just that within us!

As *God Calling* puts it, "Think of My trees—stripped of their beauty, pruned, cut, disfigured, bare, but through the dark seemingly dead branches, flows silently, secretly, the spirit-life-sap, till, lo! with the sun of spring comes new life, leaves, bud, blossom, fruit, but oh! fruit a thousand times better for the pruning.

What would our spouse or best friend say about our fruit?

IS OUR FRUIT SWEET AND OTHERS ARE NOURISHED AND REFRESHED BY IT, OR ARE WE NEGATIVE, PITHY AND HARD TO DIGEST? ARE WE PROFESSING TO BE CHRISTIANS BUT THE WORLD OBSERVES THAT WE ARE STRESSED OUT, HAVE A LACK OF SELF CONTROL AND ARE SAD SACKS? Our confession should match our behavior!

Do you know what astounds an unbeliever? It's a believer at ease under pressure!

Life with God is not immunity from difficulties, but peace *in* difficulties.

In difficult situations, are we able to do what we know to do and *trust God with the outcome?*

Have you tossed, flung, hurled, cast, pitched, thrown all your troubles (both big and small) into God's red wagon, and went off skipping happily and carefree like a trusting child, knowing with full assurance that God was handling them? The strain comes when we are carrying two days' burden on the one day.

I want to give you a little secret. If my problems are too big for God, then who do I think I am to be able to handle them? Truth in fact is, if God can't manage and control all that concerns me, then I am sunk! I will declare, "When I am afraid, I will put my trust in God." Psa. 56:3. NAS. Just stand still and hold firm during the storms, and follow directions given! Incidentally, waiting is some of the hardest work we can do.

GOD HAS NO LIMITS WHATEVER--ONLY THE LIMITS WE PUT ON HIM!

THE PERSON OF THE HOLY SPIRIT

Chapter 12

THE HOLY SPIRIT GIVES GIFTS

The Holy Spirit Gives Us Gifts.

In this last chapter, let's concentrate on inviting the Holy Spirit into our hearts and lives, letting Him take control of what we need. Let's not focus on one or two particular gifts to the exclusion of the other 22. The Holy Spirit is God himself and He will handle the gift giving. Why does man always insist on writing his own interpretation of what the Holy Spirit wrote? Man usually writes to accommodate his own theology.

The gifts of the Holy Spirit are meaningless without the fruit of the Holy Spirit (*mainly without love*). "If I had the gift of prophecy and knew all about what is going to happen in the future, knew everything about everything, but didn't love others, what good would it do? Even if I had the gift of faith so that I could speak to a mountain and make it move, I would still be worth nothing at all without love. If I gave everything I have to poor people, and if I were burned alive for preaching the Gospel but didn't love others, it would be of no value whatever." I Cor. 13:1,3.

Every believer is equipped with some gift, given to each person by the Holy Spirit as He chooses for the common good of all. I Cor. 12:1-11.

GLORY CHAPMAN

Six separate lists of gifts appear in the New Testament:

WORD OF WISDOM
WORD OF KNOWLEDGE
FAITH
GIFTS OF HEALING
WORKING OF MIRACLES
PROPHECY
DISCERNING OF SPIRITS
TONGUES
INTERPRETATION OF TONGUES   I Cor. 12:8-10

APOSTLE
PROPHECY
TEACHING
MIRACLES
HEALINGS
HELPS
ADMINISTRATION
TONGUES   I Cor. 12:28

APOSTLE
PROPHECY
TEACHING
MIRACLES
HEALING
TONGUES
INTERPRETATION OF TONGUES   I Cor. 12:29-30

PROPHECY
SERVING

THE PERSON OF THE HOLY SPIRIT

TEACHING
EXHORTATION
GIVING
LEADING
MERCY   Romans 12:6-8

APOSTLE
PROPHECY
EVANGELISM
PASTOR/TEACHER   Eph. 4:11

SPEAKING
SERVING   I Peter 4:11

In our day, tongues seem to be the most talked about subject of the Holy Spirit. Why focus on only *one* gift? Do we discard and dismiss the Holy Spirit based on some misuse and misunderstanding of only one gift out of some 22 gifts? We better think again about who we are dismissing! The Pharisees dismissed Jesus also. The counterfeit never validates the truth: The truth validates the truth!

Paul says, Pursue love, yet desire earnestly spiritual gifts, but especially that you may *prophesy*. For one who speaks in a tongue does not speak to men, but to God; for no one understands, but in his spirit he speaks mysteries. But one who prophesies speaks to men for edification and exhortation and consolation. One who speaks in a tongue edifies himself; but one who prophesies edifies the church. . . .and greater is one who prophesies than one who speaks in tongues unless he interprets, so that the church may receive edifying." I Cor. 14:1-5 NAS.

"But if there is no interpreter, let him keep silent in the church; and let him speak to himself and to God." I Cor. 14:28. NAS.

"For no prophecy recorded in Scripture was ever thought up by the prophet himself. It was the Holy Spirit within these godly men who gave them true messages from God." 2 Peter 2:20-21.

All the gifts are important as it says, but some bless the entire church. **We are to greatly desire the best gifts--not only for the gifts per se, but for the giver of the gifts--- the person of the Holy Spirit, who is God and very Jesus---**who will give us what He decides. *Fall in love with a person, not a gift, and it will all fall into proper order!*

"The Holy Spirit displays God's power through each of us as a means of helping the entire church." I Cor. 12:7. When we are full and running over, we are apt to splash over onto others. When we are excited about some new book, movie, product, country, or experience, what do we do? We rush to tell our friends.

SEARCH AND ASK THE HOLY SPIRIT FOR YOUR GIFT! We are all to serve in some capacity in the family of God. And please never, never compare your gift with someone else's!

Peter says, "As each one has received a gift, minister it to

THE PERSON OF THE HOLY SPIRIT

one another, as good stewards of the manifold grace of God." 1 Peter 4:10.

What is the Greatest Response We Can Offer to the Giver of Gifts?

We can *put the gift into action.* Suppose you were given a brand new Rolls Royce as a gift, but you never drove it! The very fact you are driving it endlessly and enjoying it so much is proof of your love for the gift. There is a special niche in the family of God that only you can fill. Exercise your gift every chance you get. *The Holy Spirit will become as important to you as you allow Him to be. He won't force himself on you. He sits back quietly and waits.* Give Him control. He's not asking for rededication. He's asking for surrender. It's at the point of surrender that you begin to experience - and enjoy - the quality of the Spirit-filled life.

Let's take a moment and grade ourselves as to how much fruit is hanging on our tree!

Does our tree contain mostly leaves? Is our fruit in its blooming stage? Or is our fruit small and shriveling up? Hopefully, our fruit is plump, juicy, colorful and others are drawn to it, thereby nourished and refreshed.

Suppose for illustration purposes that we received as a gift an electric vacuum cleaner upon conversion, together with all the equipment, but we were too young, actually a baby in the family of God, and didn't know how to use the vacuum. We were given time to grow up and mature. Then we were expected to take our place in the family, and use the equipment and gifts. The vacuum is all there, but there is no knowledge as to its operation. *The Holy Spirit is our power source who will teach and help us as to how to use the vacuum or the gift given to us.* Could it be possible that some of us will stand before the Judgment Seat of Christ with only our initial gift? We never plugged into the source of power to change us or our world, nor discovered what we were to do with the vacuum or gift!

At some point in our Christian walk, it is imperative that we ask for help.

"If you then, being evil, know how to give good gifts to your children, how much more shall your heavenly Father give the Holy Spirit to those who ask Him?" Luke 11:13 NAS.

Paul speaking to the Christians at Ephesus said, "Don't drink too much wine, for many evils lie along that path; be *filled* instead with the Holy Spirit, and *controlled* by him." Eph. 4:18 If we can be full, can we also go on empty sometimes?

Do we not need more than one bath to be refreshed, or more than one meal to be nourished? It is an ongoing and continuous need we have. Daily!

Remember the story about the talents: 5, 2 and 1? They all received talents, but what did they do with them? The 5 became 10; the two became 4; but the man with only one talent, went and hid it because he knew the Lord was a

THE PERSON OF THE HOLY SPIRIT

hard master. *What are we doing with our gift?* If we don't use our gift, it will be taken from us and given to the one who has the most.

"But his master replied, 'Wicked man' Lazy slave! . . .Take the money from this man and give it to the man with the ten talents. For the man who uses well what he is given shall be given more, and he shall have abundance. But from the man who is unfaithful, even what little responsibility he has shall be taken from him. And throw the useless servant out into outer darkness; there shall be weeping and gnashing of teeth." Matt. 25:26-30.

Don't ever insult the Holy Spirit by thinking your gift is unimportant.

He has given you exactly the gifts He wants you to have. 1 Cor. 12:11: "It is the same and only Holy Spirit who gives all these gifts and powers, deciding which each one of us should have."

I knew a woman who received a diamond ring from her husband for Christmas. Upon unwrapping the gift, she threw it across the floor saying it was too small. They are now divorced.

The function of any church should be to expect, identify and awaken the varied gifts that sleep within the community of believers. Each gift is important.

"Since you are so anxious to have special gifts from the Holy Spirit, ask him for the very best, for those that will be of real help to the whole church." I Cor. 14:12.

The Holy Spirit Baptizes Believers Into the Body of Christ.

". . .For by one Spirit we were all baptized into one body--whether Jews or Greeks, whether slaves or free--and have all been made to drink into one Spirit." 1 Cor. 12:13. KJV. Even though we may have only one gift, we are a valuable part of the body. The Holy Spirit distributes spiritual gifts to each one individually as *He wills.* 1 Cor. 12:11.

The Holy Spirit Anoints Us to Ministry.

We need to be sure we're following the leading of the Holy Spirit and serving where He has appointed and anointed us. For a fuller understanding of what to be anointed means, turn to the last pages of this book. At the moment of belief God anoints each believer with the Holy Spirit so that like Christ, he may glorify God by his life. Matt. 5:16. **Get ready!**

"You made all the delicate, inner parts of my body, and knit them together in my mother's womb. Thank you for making me so wonderfully complex! It is amazing to think about. Your workmanship is marvelous--and how well I know it. You were there while I was being formed in utter seclusion! You saw me before I was born and **SCHEDULED EACH DAY OF MY LIFE BEFORE I BEGAN TO BREATHE. EVERY DAY WAS RECORDED IN YOUR BOOK!** How precious it is, Lord, to realize that you are thinking about me constantly!

THE PERSON OF THE HOLY SPIRIT

I can't even count how many times a day your thoughts turn towards me. And when I waken in the morning, you are still thinking of me!" Psalms 139:13,18.

Are we on schedule as God planned our purpose for being born?

God put me on the earth to accomplish a certain number of things. Right now I'm so far behind, I will never die!

The Holy Spirit Gives Direction to Our Lives.

It is vital that we hear His voice. Part of the problem with the churches mentioned in the book of Revelation was that they were no longer sensitive to the direction of the Holy Spirit. The Holy Spirit can cause better things to happen to us than we can. *He has our best interest at heart and in accordance with the will of God.*

Read Acts 8:29; 10:19,20; 11:12; 13:2-4; 16:6; 19:21--all about specific instructions given them.

THE HOLY SPIRIT WILL CHANGE:

The way we hear, speak, our appearance, behavior, position, vision, discernment, attitude, tradition, outlook, prayer life, our calling, our authority, be a partner in decision making, change our direction, change our world, change our understanding, change us as His presence lingers upon us, change our leadership, change our insight, change our commission, increase our influence, establish our eternal hope, give us great confidence, change our witness, change our chaos into peace, and change our conflict into victory

Make the Holy Spirit Welcome in Your Heart.

Each morning, invite Him in afresh for each new day, making ourselves available to Him. He knows if we are wholehearted in our invitation, or only wanting Him to solve some problem or crisis for us!

If the Holy Spirit is the only person of the Godhead available to us in this world, and we ignore, grieve, quench, insult, and resist Him, who else will help us?

IS IT POSSIBLE TO BYPASS THE HOLY SPIRIT AND GO DIRECT TO GOD THE FATHER OR JESUS CHRIST? Good question!

Sort of like going to your mother for financial help, and insulting your father who has all the funds!

Can you believe after learning about the person of the Holy Spirit that anyone would not want Him to be their best friend? Everyone would except we have an enemy who works tirelessly on our unbelief and deceives us by well disguised ploys. Otherwise, we wouldn't be deceived!

What can be more important than getting to know the person of the Holy Spirit, who in actuality is God Himself? Which kingdom are we serving and putting our energy and faith into? It's our decision and choice! I have news for you though--there is but one other kingdom and the ruler there

THE PERSON OF THE HOLY SPIRIT

has death and destruction in mind for you.

Do you have a feeling you know what God would have you do, but you really don't want to face it? Ask the Holy Spirit for His assistance. He can act on your behalf in a powerfully awesome and loving manner with your best interest in mind and bring you to an incredibly beautiful eternal home. He will share all of his glorious creation with you, which is beyond description. Can we even conceive of such a perfect and honest government? He will rule and reign in love and righteousness *forever*.

The most important thing is not to try to dissect and analyze when, where, how, who and what others do about the Holy Spirit. We need to accept fully and completely His person into our own hearts and become very close friends. He will certainly take care of His work if we will trust and turn to Him with our whole heart. He can be trusted totally because He is God and very Jesus. He desires that we be *full* of the Holy Spirit and *power* at all times. Remember, no one can hinder our inner worship between the Holy Spirit and us!

The words of Jesus ring loud and clear, "Heaven and earth will pass away, but my words shall not pass away." Matt. 24:35 NAS

GLORY CHAPMAN

GLORY CHAPMAN

ANOINTED

ANOINT describes the procedure of rubbing or smearing a person or thing, usually with oil, for the purpose of healing, setting apart, or embalming. The Hebrew verb *mashach (noun, messiah)* and the Greek verb *chrio (noun, christos)* are translated t*o anoint.* From ancient times the priests and kings were ceremonially anointed as a sign of official appointment to office, and as a symbol of God's power upon them. The act was imbued with an element of awe. David would not harm King Saul because of the anointing the king had received (I Sam. 24:6). Israel came to see each succeeding king as God's anointed one, the Messiah who would deliver them from their enemies and establish the nation as God's presence on the earth.

Luke 4:18: The Spirit of the Lord is upon Me, Because He anointed Me to preach the gospel to the poor. He has sent Me to proclaim release to the captives, and recovery of sight to the blind, to set free those who are downtrodden, to proclaim the favorable year of the Lord. (This is a quote from the book of Isaiah). NAS

Isaiah 10:27: And it shall come to pass in that day, that his burden shall be taken away from off thy shoulder, and his yoke from off thy neck, and the yoke shall be destroyed because of the anointing.

Christians see Jesus as God's Anointed One, the Savior. The same symbolism as in the Old Testament is employed in this usage: God's presence and power are resident in the anointing.

THE PERSON OF THE HOLY SPIRIT

At the moment of belief God *anoints* each believer with the Holy Spirit so that like Christ (Christos means *the Anointed One*), he may glorify God by his life. (Matt. 5:16).

"Now He who establishes us with you in Christ and anointed us is God who also sealed us and gave us the Spirit in our hearts as a pledge." 2 Cor. 1:21,22.

John wrote that believers receive this anointing from God. (I John 2:20,26). It is a pouring out of the Holy Spirit on the believer, reminiscent of the anointing of priests with oil.

"And as for you, the anointing which you received from Him abides in you, and you have no need for anyone to teach you; but as His anointing teaches you about all things, and is true and is not a lie, and just as it has taught you, you abide in Him." I John 2:27.

A further consequence of the Spirit's presence is the seal of ownership, which also is accomplished at the moment of faith. Eph.1:13,14. A seal on a document in New Testament times identified it and indicated its owner, who would *protect* it. So too, in salvation, the Holy Spirit, like a seal, confirms that Christians are identified with Christ and are God's property, protected by Him. I Cor. 6:19,20.

A third work of the Spirit at salvation is His confirmation that what God has begun He will complete. Present redemption is only a foretaste of what eternity holds (Rom. 8:23)